# HOMECOMING

# HOMECOMING

Overcome Fear and Trauma
to Reclaim Your Whole, Authentic Self

## Thema Bryant, PhD

A TarcherPerigee Book

**tarcher**perigee

An imprint of Penguin Random House LLC
penguinrandomhouse.com

Most TarcherPerigee books are available at special quantity discounts for bulk purchase for sales promotions, premiums, fund-raising, and educational needs. Special books or book excerpts also can be created to fit specific needs. For details, write: SpecialMarkets@penguinrandomhouse.com.

Hardcover ISBN: 9780593418314
Ebook ISBN: 9780593418338

Printed in the United States of America
1st Printing

Book design by Laura K. Corless

Dedicated to my children Ife and Ayo, my love and joy.
May you always be at home within yourself wherever you are.
If you ever find yourself wandering away from your own voice, heart, spirit,
may you have the courage and support to find your way back.
My love for you is unconditional. May your love for yourself be the same.
You are worthy.

*Surely goodness and mercy will follow you all the days of your life.*

—PSALM 23:6

# CONTENTS

INTRODUCTION
Homesick and Disconnected                                          ix


## PART ONE
### Longing for Home

CHAPTER ONE
Ring the Alarm: I Need a Homecoming                                  3

CHAPTER TWO
Internal Signs of Disconnection                                     13

CHAPTER THREE
External Signs of Disconnection                                     31


## PART TWO
### Packing Light: What to Carry on the Journey Home

CHAPTER FOUR
Reparenting Yourself                                                53

CHAPTER FIVE
Emotional Intelligence                                             71

CHAPTER SIX
Community Care and Self-Care                                       89

CHAPTER SEVEN
Building Self-Confidence 107

CHAPTER EIGHT
Spiritual Practices 123

## PART THREE
### Recovering from Roadblocks on the Journey Home

CHAPTER NINE
Mourning Invisible Losses 145

CHAPTER TEN
Healing from Breakups and Divorce 159

CHAPTER ELEVEN
Coping and Healing from a Toxic Workplace 173

CHAPTER TWELVE
Recovering from Childhood Trauma 189

CHAPTER THIRTEEN
Resisting Oppression 203

CONCLUSION
Welcome Home: The Journey Continues 219

ADDITIONAL RESOURCES 225

ACKNOWLEDGMENTS 229

# Homesick and Disconnected

*In West Africa, the story is told of an animal expert. This expert knew every animal in the bush. In America, you say* forest, *but the real word is* bush. *One day, as this expert was walking, he passed a farm. In the back of the farm, he saw so so*[*] *chickens, and in the middle of the chickens was an eagle. The man was vexed to see the eagle acting like a chicken. He went to the front of the farm and knocked on the farmer's door.*

*He said, "Bop bop." In America you say* knock, knock, *but the real sound is* bop bop. *The man inside said, "Who that?" The man outside said, "That me. You must open the door and see."*

*The farmer opened the door and said, "What's your business here?" The man outside said, "I'm an animal expert, and I see that behind your farm, you have so so chickens, but in the middle is one eagle."*

*The farmer said, "No, I don't have any eagles. Only chickens." The expert said, "Let me show you."*

---

* *So so* is a Liberian English expression for *many*.

*They walked to the back of the farm, and the expert picked up the eagle and said, "Listen to me. You're an eagle. You can fly. They're chickens. They can't fly. So go now and fly."*

*The eagle looked at the man and then looked down at his chicken brothers and sisters eating their chicken food. He hopped off the man's arm and started eating the food. The farmer laughed at the expert and said, "I told you. I don't have any eagles." The expert was shamed and vexed. He said, "I'm coming to go."*

*He left the farm. The next day he came back so early in the morning that God was not awake yet. He knocked at the farmer's door. The farmer was frustrated but let him in. He walked to the back of the farm and picked up the eagle. He climbed on top of the barn. He told the eagle, "All your life people have treated you like chicken. They taught you to talk like chicken and eat like chicken and think like chicken, but you're not a chicken. You're an eagle. You can fly now, so fly."*

*At that moment the sun started to rise. The animal expert said, "You see how far that sun is? You can go there. Now fly." The eagle thought, "This man will come bother me every day until I try this thing, so let me try." He stretched his wings, and my people, you have never seen such a beautiful sight. The eagle flew toward the sun, and the farmer never saw him again.*

The eagle made it home. He made it back to the truth of who he was. This is homecoming. I wrote this book for all of you who at different points in your life have found yourself living like someone you are not. You may have started acting different because of how you were treated, or what other people told you about yourself, or how you saw others acting. You have not felt comfortable or safe enough to truly be yourself or to feel at home in your identity. The recognized and unrecognized traumas of your past may have taught you to hide your gifts and voice in order to survive.

This book facilitates your journey back to who you really are, so you can own your full identity and fly.

As a psychologist and a minister, I enter into spaces where people have been wounded when others have tried to define, limit, or erase them. Yet I see people as much more than the sum of the injustices and invalidations they have faced. In writing this book, I have the same hopeful conviction that you can heal the wounds of your past and journey back home to your authentic self. I wrote this book because I believe each of us can live more connected and in tune with our authentic selves. Daring to live authentically is so important because you come to realize that despite the ways you may have been derailed by adversity, you can genuinely love and accept yourself. This is liberating. I am so glad a part of you believes homecoming, or living authentically, is important, too.

Your decision to show up for this process is an important step as you acknowledge the desire for a more authentic, fulfilling, and centered life. A centered life is one that is grounded in your core values rather than changing based on the most recent trend, compliment, or outside expectation. I invite you to take a sacred breath. In this moment as we start the journey, give yourself permission to become aware of the ways you may have lost sight of yourself. Homecoming begins as you set an intention to reconnect to yourself, to acknowledge and heal the disconnection so you can be your authentic self again—or for the first time. The stress and traumas of life may have disconnected you from your sense of self, your confidence, and even your thoughts and feelings. As you heal and grow, you get to a place of appreciating and honoring yourself in mind, body, heart, and spirit.

## FEELING HOMESICK

You may be homesick, longing for your psychological home, which is not based on geography or a physical living space, but your interior life—it is the ability to know, honor, appreciate, and love yourself wherever you are. You are a sacred being, worthy of care and compassion, and you are not alone. *Cojourners* is the term I use to describe our community—those who are somewhere on the journey between disconnection and reconnection, between wandering and grounded, and between homesick and homecoming. Each person reading this book along with you has had some experiences that took them off course. Those experiences may have occurred years ago during childhood or as recently as this month. There are also some who, like me, have had multiple points of disconnection. There may have been major roadblocks in your journey, or a series of potholes and speed bumps that slowed you down. Regardless of the path that led us here, we can make this journey together—the journey home to our authentic selves.

As a womanist psychologist (a liberation, decolonized psychologist, centering the voices of Black women and others who have been marginalized), I use *us* and *we* intentionally in order to honor our shared humanity. We have lived full lives that include both seasons of self-neglect and seasons of authentic homecoming. I reject the idea that mental health professionals or ministers are blank slates or all-knowing, perfect beings. I want you to remember throughout your journey that you are not alone, that there is a *we* present in this homecoming. The information in this book, combined with your wisdom and life experience, can position, guide, and nourish you for the journey home.

Like some of you, I had to make the journey home to myself on multiple occasions. During my early years growing up in Baltimore, I was teased and demeaned for having a dark complexion. This teasing was based on colorism, which I later discovered exists not only in the Black community but also among Asians and Latinos. As a result of White supremacy, many people globally have been treated better based on how close their appearance is to Whiteness. I had to actively work to resist these messages to be able to see and embrace my beauty and worth. I came home to self-acceptance in part because of my wonderful experience living in Liberia, in West Africa, during high school. While living there, I saw that every-one who was in a position of power looked like me, and this was liberating and affirming. I was at home within myself, and then devastatingly, at the end of my second year living there, a civil war broke out, and after the vio-lence escalated I was abruptly evacuated with my family and other Amer-icans back to the States, left to grieve the loss of many friends and the community that had so readily embraced me. Journaling, dance, faith, community, and therapy helped me make the journey back home to myself again. Homecoming may be a journey you take multiple times in your life. But I am here to tell you that it is possible and that you are worth every step.

I appreciate everyone on the journey and would particularly like to acknowledge those who are looking to create a life that they have never experienced. For some of you, this journey is about cultivating the kind of life you have never experienced, or you witnessed others experiencing but had doubts about whether it was possible for yourself. You may never have seen a healthy relationship modeled in your family, but you want to end that cycle. You may never have seen anyone practice healthy boundaries and self-care to protect their mental health, but you want that for your own life. You may never have experienced a sense of joy, fulfillment, or purpose in your work, but you would like to create a life where you enjoy your week and not just your weekend.

## WHAT IS A HOMECOMING?

The journey home is both psychological and spiritual. In fact, the word *psychology* means *study of the soul* as it originates from the Greek word *psyche* (soul). Often people fall into two camps based on how they have been raised or taught. Some spiritual and religious people are unwilling to ac-knowledge and address mental health. Likewise some psychologically oriented people are uncomfortable acknowledging spirituality. But the journey home requires every part of you. This is a holistic journey. We do not need to leave our minds, hearts, bodies, cultures, or spirits behind.

I grew up as a pastor's daughter and have often heard people of faith speak dismissively of therapy, mental illness, and medication. In these religious spaces, people often receive the message that faith and prayer is all that should be needed for wellness. I have also been in academic circles and medical practices where some professionals speak dismissively of faith and prayer. As a minister and psychologist, I am glad to be among those who are bridging the gaps between faith and mental health. Mental health challenges, including mental illness, exist across faith traditions. People are multidimensional and should not be made to feel that they have to choose between the diverse pathways of restoration. For that reason, *Homecoming* is a spiritual and psychological guide that will not require you to neglect any aspect of yourself.

Homecoming is sacred work in that I believe miraculous things can happen. Change, growth, and transformation can occur. In fact, I wouldn't be surprised if some miracles have already happened. For people to have lived through trauma and still have kindness, a sense of humor, compassion, dreams, and a seed of hope that their lives can be better is pretty amazing. So before we begin the journey home, honor yourself for the ways you have survived. Perhaps you have some scars, but you are here nonetheless.

The journey home is also political for members of marginalized communities. If you have faced individual and institutional barriers that have made it hard for you to be at home with yourself, this journey is a radical, revolutionary act that resists erasure, stigma, stereotype, racism, sexism, and oppression in all its forms. It is beautiful to see you setting the intention to make your way back home to yourself despite all the naysayers who have systematically tried to tell you that you were unworthy of justice, wellness, and compassion.

Your seed of hope in the possibility of being more connected to yourself, more grounded in the sacred truth of who you are, is the foundation of home. This hope involves visualizing a place of inner peace. Life's storms might have left you feeling stranded and stuck. Yet, Cojourner, you are here with us embarking on a trip of a lifetime.

## THE GENESIS OF *HOMECOMING*

In raising me and my brother, my parents emphasized the importance of engaging in community outreach and empowerment. This value of generosity and collective responsibility echoes what I later learned about Black psychology, liberation psychology, and multicultural feminist psychology. All of these approaches to psychology are based on a recognition that wellness should not just be for the elite, the wealthy, or the few. Psychologists are in positions to share knowledge beyond the academy, therapy room, or professional conventions. Psychological wellness is for all people, especially those who have been marginalized. For that reason, not only do I provide therapy and teach future psychologists at a university, but I have been intentional about connecting with community organizations to share knowledge about mental health and to learn from community members' indigenous and spiritual principles for healing and wellness. I also started *The Homecoming Podcast*, which is a mental health podcast to empower people to make the journey back home to their authentic selves. I have been honored and humbled by the international reach of the podcast and the many listeners from all walks of life who write to me to share their journey and their struggles. I hope that this book will help you in your own journey—whether you're new to this or whether you've been following along with the podcast. I am grateful that this book began with me as a little Black girl in Baltimore writing in a journal and is now manifesting in this moment where you are reading the words that come from my heart. I'm home.

## CAUTIONS ON THE JOURNEY

Some of us have been taught to arm ourselves with a toxic positivity that denies painful realities. Toxic positivity is the message that you can think and talk only about positive things. It forces people to suppress and silence their pain with the mistaken belief that if they try not to think about it, it will go away. This denial and erasure of our full human experience can give the appearance of homecoming but is yet another form of disconnection. Denial is never healing or transformative. When I cannot be honest about how I feel and what I need or want, even with myself, I am far from home. As we journey home, we recognize the ways in which we have lied to ourselves—when we have convinced ourselves that we were okay when we weren't, or when we adjusted to dysfunction and began to see problematic dynamics as routine because they had indeed become our norm. You can begin to admit to yourself the times when you were in fact miserable, angry, tired, and disappointed. Homecoming requires truth-telling—both to ourselves and to others.

I invite you to not distract yourself with busyness, and to remember that busy does not equal healed or home. I invite you to release the tendency to distract yourself with temporary fixes that often amplify the original problem. Temporary fixes may medicate the pain in the moment, but the wound remains unhealed. We can distract ourselves with food, substances, shopping, and even perpetual motion. If you have spent seasons of your life chasing goals that really do not matter to you, that do not fulfill you, this is another manifestation of being emotionally homesick. While you may grieve lost time, you can also appreciate the present moment as you begin to move in the direction of your authentic self and your dreams. You begin to reject the scripts that other people wrote for you when you recognize that those words and actions do not align with your vision for your life.

Throughout the journey, I will share parts of my story as well as accounts from others whose identities have been disguised. The stories are reminders that you are not alone in feeling disconnected or longing for a more authentic life. As you read about my journey and the other narratives, I invite you to reflect on your life story, both the roads that took you where you are now and the roads you would like to choose in the present.

## HOMEWORK

With each chapter I will provide homework to help you apply what you're reading to your life. We can all remember times when we heard a good speech, sermon, lecture, workshop, or podcast. The challenge is to move from hearing it to living it. Internalizing what you are reading requires active reflection and wellness activities. One psychological approach is called solutions-focused therapy, usually a short-term therapy for people who don't have years to dedicate to the process. In solutions-focused therapy, a part of the work you do is to look at the things that have worked for you in the past but that you have been too distracted to do because of stress and trauma, and you reinstate them. Let's consider those things now. What are the things you have done in the past that have given you a sense of peace, clarity, fulfillment, or joy? What are ways you have fed your spirit, your mind, your heart, and your body? While you and I may name some similar activities, we should also keep in mind that we are individuals, so what works for you may not work for me, and that is okay. We should not expect everyone's coping and healing journey to look identical to our journey. For some coping looks like meditation, and for others it is journaling. For some it is hiking, and for others it is karaoke. For some it is being vegan, and for others it is starting the day with prayer. While we may not all gravitate to the same things, sometimes we need to step out of our comfort zone and discover new ways to nourish ourselves.

Now begin to consider when you last did your homecoming activity—something you enjoy that brings you back to yourself. For me, it is dancing.

Dancing nourishes me spiritually, psychologically, emotionally, and physically, but when I am stressed or overwhelmed, I forget to dance. When I carve out time to dance, it brings me back to myself. Other homecoming activities include calling an authentic and loving friend or relative, decluttering your space, and listening to inspiring music. Before you jump into the next chapter, I encourage you to make a commitment to yourself to engage in one activity that reconnects you to yourself and is not destructive to your health and well-being. For example, if you think about calling a crush but realize you always get off the phone feeling unfulfilled and uncertain about how they feel about you, such a call is not your homecoming activity. If your potential homecoming activity is having your favorite food or drink, but you know that usually ends with you eating or drinking too much and feeling sick or disappointed in yourself, that is not your homecoming activity. So choose a nourishing activity that helps you to feel more connected to yourself and then decide how many times you want to do that this week. You may want to schedule the activity more frequently than is your current norm, but you also want the goal to be realistic so you don't set yourself up for failure. If you had fried chicken for dinner last night, you may not want to go vegetarian immediately. Rather, you could start with "meatless Mondays." Additionally, you want to select an activity that is in your budget. If one of the things that helps me reconnect with myself is a cruise or a massage, but I do not currently have the funds for either, I should select something else that I can access now. Your homecoming activity may bring you a greater sense of being alive. Howard Thurman, a great African American theologian, once wrote, "Don't ask what the world needs. Ask what makes you come alive, and go do it. Because what the world needs is people who have come alive."

Once you have selected and scheduled your activity, you are ready to begin. This week, practice your homecoming activity as you continue to read this book. In part 1, you will learn more about the signs of homesickness and disconnection and ways to address them. In part 2, you will learn about long-term skills and mindsets to help you come home to yourself, and in part 3, you will discover strategies for addressing the major road-blocks to your homecoming.

## ENDING OUR BEGINNING

Cojourner, I'm so glad you're on this journey with me. After everything you have survived and endured, it is my sacred honor to journey with you on your homecoming. I am grateful that you are here, and I am excited about what you will discover and recover on the journey home. I will end this chapter and every chapter with the invitation I offer at the end of each episode of *The Homecoming Podcast*:

I invite your soul to tell your heart, mind, body, and spirit, "Welcome home."

# HOMECOMING

# PART ONE

Longing for Home

# CHAPTER ONE

# Ring the Alarm: I Need a Homecoming

*There's a feeling here inside . . .*
*I wish I was home.*
—"SOON AS I GET HOME," AS SUNG
BY DIANA ROSS IN *THE WIZ*

*Home is not a place. . . . It's a feeling.*
—CECELIA AHERN

was a Black girl in Baltimore, about nine years old and still playing with dolls. The phone rang, and I answered it. The person on the other end didn't give me a chance to identify myself. There was no time to say, "This is not Pastor Bryant." The caller was already crying and halfway through her story before I could say, "Hold on a minute. Let me get my dad." This kind of call was not rare because I grew up as a pastor's daughter in a community that had more trust in and received more comfort from ministers than therapists. A few years later, when I was a teen and people would call while my parents weren't home, I would offer a listening ear or any words of comfort or assurance that came to mind. I guess you could say my first time working on a crisis hotline was in my home as a teen. I appreciated these moments of bearing witness and being present with people as they tried to navigate the valleys of life. I had already experienced some valleys myself and understood the value of being heard, seen, and supported.

When I learned that this was not just a role for pastors, but that for some people this was their life's work, I made the decision to become a psychologist.

As a psychologist, I have worked for over twenty years with diverse people who had a range of concerns, from workplace stress to family conflict. As a social-justice-oriented therapist, I am mindful that many of the challenges people face do not originate solely within them. Systemic oppression and biases influence our lives in critical ways that can affect our mental health. I love being a psychologist—for me, it transcends the limits of a career. It is a vocation, a sacred calling to facilitate the process of healing.

Whether working to help people cope with daily sources of stress or major life events, I have found the most challenging persons to work with are those who don't want to be in therapy and don't see any need to grow, heal, or change. One's motivation for change greatly influences the experience one has in therapy. Lack of motivation is especially evident when I think about clients I have worked with who were mandated to attend therapy by a judge or who were required to come by a spouse or parent. These clients did not see a problem with themselves or with the way they were living. One of the first things I have to do in such sessions—whether with an abusive spouse, someone with substance use disorder, or an argumentative teenager—is address motivation. When clients are not willing to engage, they will attempt to spend the entire session talking about why they don't need to be there, how great everything is, or even what is happening on their favorite television show. We have to do the work of motivation before we can begin the deeper work.

Your decision to pick up this book means that you have recognized one or more areas in which you want to grow, and you already have some motivation to enhance your life. I'm glad that something about the idea of homecoming resonated with you. Let me first paint for you a clear picture of homecoming. *Homecoming is a return to authentic living that is based on truth, self-acceptance, and an aligning of action with values and purpose.* Home is more than a physical location; it is an emotional and spiritual space of belonging, appreciation, and love. When I am at home within myself, I have nothing to prove. I am free to be myself without pretense or performance. Homecoming is moving away from the detours and disconnections and coming back to the wisdom housed in our hearts, minds, bodies, and spirits. Dr. Maya Angelou said, "I long, as does every human being, to be at home wherever I find myself. The ache for home lives in all of us."

To decide I need a homecoming means I have recognized that there are some ways in which I have been living disconnected or unaware of myself, my needs, my wounds, my knowledge, or even my dreams. So if you feel disconnected from yourself, the question arises: "Who or what has been dictating your life?" Some of you have lived out your parents' dreams and expectations. Some of you have lived in reaction to people who have hurt you, causing you to build a life based on revenge or the idea that you have to "show them" that you are valuable, important, or enough. Still others have constructed an identity and life to gain the approval of friends and even strangers, without ever checking in to see if you approve of yourself.

*Rain, a Latina in her late twenties, feels stuck in her resentment. She is angry about what she did not receive as a child. The way her family mistreated and emotionally neglected her was hurtful, and she has faced many consequences from the pain of those formative years. The problem with being stuck looking back is that you never get to live in the present. The problem with focusing all of your attention on the people who let you down is that you can let yourself down by not paying attention to your own needs. Rain joins us on this journey, recognizing the signs that she is not at home with herself. She is ready to come home, to give herself what she never received.*

While a handful of you may have picked up this book after one week of disconnection, most of us have gone through extended periods when we were not tuned into our thoughts and feelings. We can lose ourselves, subtly and slowly, without even realizing it. Those around us may not have noticed, either. Losing track of yourself while you take care of others may even be encouraged by your culture, religion, social circle, or professional field. An awakening to the reality of your disconnection is necessary to begin the journey home. This chapter will highlight some of the thought patterns and emotional weights that are signs that you have been living with some level of disconnection from yourself. I will provide you with the empowering skills to recognize these signs, and I'll offer some initial tips to begin charting the course back home to yourself. Recognizing and addressing these internal signs is important because not only is living an inauthentic life unfulfilling, but it can also become harmful to your physical and mental health.

*If I didn't define myself for myself,*
*I would be crunched into other people's*
*fantasies for me and eaten alive.*
—AUDRE LORDE

What are the ways you have been crunched, boxed in, or pressured by other people's ideas about who you are or what you are supposed to be?

When were the seasons in your life when you felt overwhelmed by the opinions of others to the point that it crowded out the sound of the still small voice within?

You are not alone in this experience. The details and context vary, but many of us have had seasons or lifetimes of disconnection from ourselves.

*Charisma, a single African American woman, has felt disconnected from herself for the majority of her life. She grew up in an impoverished neighborhood where she had to be vigilant at all times. Her life vacillated between painfully silent and painfully loud. During the week, her teachers demanded constant silence in her overcrowded classrooms. Her father rarely came to see her and her mom had to work long hours, so Charisma was often home alone, focusing on schoolwork and house chores; the background noise of a television series did not reflect her reality. On the weekends, she would stay at her aunt's home, where many relatives, friends, and strangers were constantly coming and going. There was love and chaos, warmth and the constant whirl of opinions—the opinions of adults, that is. Children were not to involve themselves in grown folks' conversation. Charisma used to keep a journal, but one of her cousins took it and read its embarrassing contents to anyone who would listen. Charisma decided in that moment, when no one defended or comforted her, to keep everything locked inside. The challenge was that she became so good at locking everything away that she even locked it away from herself. Years somehow slipped past her, and now she is in her thirties—uncertain about what she feels, doubtful of what she can do, and unsure of what she knows. As she looks at the unfulfilling landscape of her years, Charisma realizes the thing she is missing is herself. She is ready for a homecoming.*

## THE JOURNEY HOME

As you come home to yourself, you begin breaking free from the mandates and dictates of others. Should-dos are the instructions that you have received from those around you or from the larger society. You may have received should-dos from your family, your teachers, the media, your friends, people you admire, and even people who despise you. We are bombarded with so many messages that tell us that because we belong to a particular family, community, race, gender, religion, age group, or whatever, we are supposed to live a certain way. Some parts of these scripts may resonate with us, while other parts don't ring true. As you shed the weight of other people's expectations and demands for your life, time, and resources, you come home to a life that resonates with, awakens, and animates you.

You have come to a place in your life when tolerance is not enough, just getting by is not enough, staying in the lane that others have forced you into is not enough. Homecoming is about living fully, abundantly, and taking up space—not adjusting to a life of dissatisfaction and discontent. I invite you to declare today, "I refuse to participate in the silencing of myself. I do not consent to the erasing of myself." As you begin this journey, you recognize how dangerous and costly it has been to live seasons of your life feeling disconnected from yourself. It has cost you self-respect, time, possibilities, and even your physical and mental health. As you come home, you have the opportunity to gain yourself back. So as you work your way through this process, the motivation, the goal, the inspiration is you. The truth is that you may have been waiting for a long time to be seen, to be appreciated, to be heard, to be loved. Coming home to yourself is giving yourself the things you have been waiting for, the things you thought only others could give you, and the things you thought you could never receive.

As Diana Ross sang in *Mahogany*, "Do you know where you're going to? / Do you like the things that life's been showing you?" These are important questions. As Bishop Vashti McKenzie, the first woman bishop in the African Methodist Episcopal Church, declared, "We're all going somewhere, but where is the somewhere of your going?" Many of us have spent years distancing ourselves from ourselves, but with each chapter of this book and each decision, we aim to make our homecoming the destination of our journey.

I invite you to take a sacred pause now and ask yourself where you're going. A sacred pause means taking a moment to breathe and check in with the silenced or ignored parts of yourself. What road have you been following based on your investment of time, money, and relationships? Where does this road lead? Is that where you want to go? I invite you to go within, instead of letting others be your compass. Sometimes people make decisions by popular vote among their friends and family. Instead, I invite you to awaken your internal compass, so you can begin to know what you feel, think, need, want, and dream. The only way to change directions is to start by being honest with yourself about the ways you have felt lost, disconnected, unfulfilled, or stuck.

To begin the journey, can you admit to yourself that you miss you? Do you miss living free from the heavy cloak of shame or grief? Do you miss sleeping through the night? Do you miss having an appetite without being consumed with emotional eating? Do you miss your laugh? Do you miss being yourself? I invite you to shatter the silence and speak truth with the words *I miss me.* Then breathe in through your nose and out through your mouth. Notice the movement in your chest, rib cage, and abdomen as you take a breath. It is healing to be missed.

Some of you may miss the person you were never free to be. If you grew up with constant trauma and stress, you may never have been able to be at home with yourself, to be free from shame, and to experience healthy eating and sleeping. We will explore trauma and other major roadblocks in greater detail in part 3. If you miss the person you never were able to be, you too have experienced homesickness—a longing to connect with yourself as you never have been safe enough to do before.

Once you acknowledge being disconnected from yourself, you begin to recognize all of the ways you have been distracted from this longing for home—with constant television watching, social media scrolling, pursuing people, smoking, drinking, shopping, or even taking on extra projects to fill your time and focus. As you come home to yourself, you release the need for perpetual external engagement so you can sit with yourself and learn to enjoy your own company. You realize that if you always need to be high or constantly have to have someone else around, you are not truly at home with yourself.

You may also begin to notice the ways you have betrayed yourself through procrastination, neglecting your needs and abandoning your dreams. It may have seemed noble or necessary at one point. You recognize this self-betrayal not to beat yourself up but to wake yourself up. While you were taking care of others, who was taking care of you? Do you want to reclaim the forgotten, neglected, betrayed parts of yourself?

When you recognize that stress and trauma led you to distraction and self-abandonment, your attention shifts from worrying about everyone else to seeing the unrecognized gift of yourself. You begin to say, "Not only do I miss myself, but I also want to get back to me. I want to rediscover my wings. I want to hear my unfiltered roar—my true voice. I want to awaken my dormant gifts."

You have become aware that you are really longing for the authentic you. You may have discovered this quickly in your youth, or you may have taken the long way home. Whatever your age, I celebrate you for recognizing the things you have been chasing and prioritizing that took you further away from yourself and did not bring lasting fulfillment. You are ready to release the *if only*. Remember when you thought you would be happy if only you could accomplish the following?

- Finish school
- Make a certain amount of money
- Get a job that your family respected
- Get married
- Have children
- Own a beautiful home
- Be respected by people who once rejected you

For those of you who haven't attained these markers, I want you to know that some people have the things you want and still are not at home with themselves. They may have received many accolades and reached all the major milestones, but somewhere on the journey, they left themselves behind. Regardless of what we have accomplished externally, we are all here for what we want to gain psychologically and spiritually, and that is ourselves. What a beautiful journey to embark upon!

*Maybe home is somewhere I'm going and never have been before.*
—WARSAN SHIRE

*I believe wherever dreams dwell, the heart calls it home.*
*So may you untangle yourself from the twist of melancholy and*
*let your thoughts carry you back to the birthplace of your trust.*
—DODINSKY

## The Beginning

We stand in this place of scattered pieces,
Seeing memories of our lives reflected in the broken glass,
Tears on faces or stuffed in pockets,
Roars and whispers locked in rib cages
Slightly moving with shallow breath.
Holding certainty in our mind and questions in our heart, we arrive
At this place that we have called home.
But we realize the walls don't match
The original design.
Our feet are hungry for earth,
Our ears await the sound of our authentic voice,
Tired of walking on this narrow trail based on the map others have
     drawn for us.
Then up from the belly,
we hear the alarm:
This isn't me.
This isn't me.
As the alarm reaches our hearts we take off,
Sometimes running, sometimes walking, sometimes stretching,
But always heading home,
Detours and all.
We are heading Home.

This is a good moment for us to take a sacred pause, a moment for intentional, unhurried full breath and reflection.

## HOMEWORK

After you read these directions, I invite you to close your eyes if that feels comfortable for you and imagine yourself when you are emotionally and spiritually at home with yourself. What will it look like? How will you breathe, speak, move through life, make decisions, love, manifest your purpose, and rest? When you are at home with yourself, what will your laugh sound like? What scent will you wear? What will shift within you and around you? Begin to get a picture of yourself at home. Allow this image to motivate you as you begin this journey, even if the image changes as you read further.

I invite your soul to tell your heart, mind, body, and spirit, "Welcome home."

# CHAPTER TWO

# Internal Signs of Disconnection

*I was standing in a crowded conference hall, giving the keynote address, wearing a fancy suit from my mother, who embodies fashion royalty, and doing what I love: talking to people about the healing journey home to their authentic selves. The conference was about sexual assault, and in my keynote, I talked about the recovery process based on my experience as a researcher, a practitioner who has helped others heal, and a sexual assault survivor myself. I ended the speech feeling inspired as I looked out over the sea of people committed to ending sexual violence. Most people came up to me with big smiles on their faces, some with tears in their eyes, but one woman stood out. I noticed her from a distance because of the disturbed look on her face. When she got to me, I took a breath and prepared to hear what she wanted to share. She looked at me with skepticism and said with disbelief, "So you're a survivor?! You don't look like any survivor I've ever seen." I held the space for silence to do the work. She stood with her question, and I stood in my truth, and then she said, "Every survivor I know is fat or on drugs or homeless like me." I opened my hands and let my eyes do the talking. She grabbed my hands and began to weep.*

*I let her see under the layers of degrees, pantsuit, PowerPoint presentation, and oratorical skills. I let her see me: a survivor.*

I am aware that many of you on this homecoming journey may not have a lot of outward signs of disconnection. However, homecoming is a matter of the heart. It is not about the appearance of things, but about how you feel—the condition of your spirit and the inner workings of your mind. You can have the résumé, relationship, and social media posts that look like happiness but still be unfulfilled.

In this chapter, we will unpack some of the emotional signs of disconnection from self, including depression, anxiety, resentment, and envy. I will provide some initial tools to empower you to access your feelings so you can continue on the journey home.

## WHY AM I DISCONNECTED?

Let's take a moment to reflect on the reasons why we disconnect from our feelings. Sometimes the pressure, stress, and demands of life are so great that we feel like we don't have time for our emotions.

Many of us were raised to dismiss our feelings based on teachings around our gender, race, and religion. Boys and men are often discouraged from showing emotions (besides anger). This requirement to shut down emotions includes not only sadness and fear but also joy. This messaging has limited many men by restricting them to define and measure their manhood by their ability to disconnect. Difficulty recognizing and expressing emotions in healthy ways is a major barrier to living authentically.

As an African American child, I can remember often hearing the phrase *Fix your face!* or *Stop all that crying before I give you something to cry about,* whether said to me or other children in reference to the threat of a beating. Children usually were not permitted to display negative emotions. It was unacceptable to look angry, sad, disappointed, bored, or frustrated. Historical enslavement and mass incarceration have led many Black parents to fear raising children who are weak or disrespectful. Survival for Black people in America has necessitated the mastery of masking emotions of discontent in particular. I know that Black Americans are not alone; other communities of color have also emphasized the importance of masking emotion, showing strength, honoring the reputation of their family and community, and enduring without complaint. While survival is important, the suppression of our feelings comes with a cost. Unhealed wounds and unresolved grief show up in destructive and unhealthy ways.

Religious and spiritual teachings have also been used as tools of suppression. Certain emotions are labeled as sin or evidence of one's lack of faith. This can lead to toxic positivity or toxic spirituality, in which human emotions are unacceptable. People are taught erroneously that if they experience uncomfortable feelings like anxiety, sadness, and anger, this means they are not grateful enough, spiritual enough, or trusting enough of God. As a result of struggling to contain these emotions, people can experience shame, which amplifies their distress and self-judgment.

In addition to teachings around gender, race, and religion, experiences of trauma can give the impression that emotions are dangerous. For people who have lived through trauma, witnessing others' anger, frustration, or irritation can be triggering. To avoid this, survivors may try to constantly keep everyone around them appeased. They can also experience a fear of disappointment, which robs them of potentially enjoyable moments because they worry that these won't last. As a result, many of us are emotionally shut down and incapable of celebrating our successes.

Whatever the cause, detachment from our emotions has become so much the norm that when we ask people how they are feeling, the socially acceptable response is "fine." In religious circles, the appropriate response is often "I'm blessed." We can absolutely be blessed and still experience sadness, worry, and frustration. In addition to hiding our emotions from others, we can also deny our emotions to ourselves, for fear of drowning in those feelings.

I was talking to a dear friend on the phone about some bad medical news she had received when she said, "I have been fighting all day to keep from crying." I asked, "What if you stop fighting and let the tears come?" She was afraid that if she let herself cry, she would lose it, and she couldn't afford to lose it because she had to be mentally prepared to fight the illness. Although we were in two different cities, we decided to leave our houses at the same time and go for a walk while talking on the phone. As we walked, she allowed the tears to come and was able to share her fears about possibly having to fight cancer in the middle of a pandemic. Walking allowed her to relieve some of the tension she was experiencing in her body, so with no one there to see her vulnerability and a good sister-friend on the phone, she felt safe enough to cry. This release created space for her to be nourished, to be comforted, and to have her needs for expression and connection met.

Some of us become emotionally shut down from exhaustion. If you have faced recurring hopelessness, powerlessness, or confusion, you may have learned to check out as a coping mechanism that has now become your automatic, unconscious response. You may be in a place where nothing, or very little, fazes you. Psychologists sometimes refer to this as dissociation, or the freeze response (as in fight, flight, or freeze). People may experience you as hard, heartless, cold, inaccessible, distant, or strong. You may have become so used to telling people that you're fine and even believing that you're fine that you're not sure when exactly things within you fell apart. The disconnection can be a way of protecting yourself from the vulnerability of feeling.

Stress or trauma leaves others unable to regulate or contain their emotions. You may often feel overwhelmed, or you may have labeled yourself as sensitive or "too much." You may be so in tune with the suffering within and around you that it is difficult to contain or communicate what you feel. Feeling things deeply and being criticized for it may have led you to build walls. I want you to know that a part of the homecoming journey is being able to express and honor your feelings.

When we are emotionally disconnected, we can neglect our needs and make decisions that aren't in alignment with our heart and our values. We may sabotage our relationships with a lack of communication, transparency, or affection. Others may assume that we don't care or that we don't need anything because we seem unmoved. Some of us learned to remain hyper-focused on the feelings of others while neglecting our own emotions in order to survive. This prevents us from setting healthy boundaries and from even being aware of our needs, wants, and feelings. Emotional intelligence is about being aware of our own feelings—not just the emotions of others—and being able to regulate and communicate our feelings. Conversely, those of us who become overwhelmed by our emotions can have difficulty tuning into the feelings of others. To come home is to be able to hear my heart's song without its being drowned out by the songs of others, and to be able to hear the songs of others without assuming their songs are the same as ours.

Emotional disconnection can come with increased risk of harm or self-deception because it is harder to pay attention to our internal alarm. With a muted alarm, we may neglect our own care, rest, hunger, and even the need to exit toxic jobs or unfulfilling relationships. A part of our homecoming is healing the wounds that have caused us to disconnect so we can awaken to our emotional consciousness.

## WHAT DO YOU LOOK LIKE WHEN YOU ARE WANDERING AND DISCONNECTED?

When you are disconnected from yourself, you may be masking and censoring yourself most of the time. You may feel that you have to appear a certain way in order to be safe, loved, chosen, or acceptable. You can easily lose sight of yourself in the process of seeking acceptance, as evidenced in Michael's story.

> *Michael is a Latino man in his thirties. He has always been the strong one in his family, group of friends, and workplace, and he is considered a natural leader. He is talented and intelligent, warm and thoughtful. He is also depressed and perfectionistic. Michael works hard but is very guarded. Many miss the fact that they do not actually know him well because he is so good at paying attention to them and giving them what they want without revealing much of himself. Michael is successful, but is always headed up the next mountain; he spends very little time appreciating and finding fulfillment in what he has achieved. Whatever he does is never enough; at his core, he believes that he is not enough.*

While psychological disconnection can manifest itself as relentless ambition in some people, it can also take the form of diminished dreams, hopes, and expectations in others. For those who have experienced depression, you may live with the anticipation of a foreshortened future or the inability to imagine yourself living beyond a set age. People who've experienced trauma often believe that their lives will be cut short early. You may have armed yourself against disappointment by always preparing for the worst, but as a result, you end up living a small, restricted life. If you are living at a fraction of your capacity, you are not at home with yourself.

Spending much of your time in toxic, draining spaces can contribute to emotional disconnection as well. If you have ever spent months or years of your life in an unhealthy relationship or a toxic workplace, you may have had to disconnect from yourself or retreat within to feel safe.

You may have been told that it is not okay to feel depressed, angry, exhausted, disappointed, lonely, or even proud of yourself. You may have received cultural and religious scripts that require masking your feelings from yourself and others. Have you ever known someone was angry, but they denied it? Have you yourself been the person who denied your feelings even when others noticed and named it? Sometimes your facial expressions, body language, and tone reveal feelings that you have not yet recognized.

Stressful and traumatic experiences may have created within you a core belief about yourself that is untrue; this keeps you disconnected from yourself. Some of these core beliefs may be:

- I am not good enough.
- I am not worthy.
- I am not lovable.
- I am not meant to have a good life.

When we believe these lies, we may mask, contort, or hide ourselves to be accepted, affirmed, and loved. We lose sight of ourselves when we spend considerable time in environments where it is not safe to be ourselves. Homecoming, however, is a refuge from life's storms—both the named and the unacknowledged.

The reality is that some people are not comfortable with your feelings. As you begin the journey home, consider the emotions that were acceptable and unacceptable to express both now and when you were growing up. Your feelings may seem inconvenient because they speak to an unmet need. You may have been shamed or ignored for your feelings, but let's make a covenant to not shame or ignore ourselves. We can instead try radical acceptance, which truly honors what we feel without fighting or pathologizing it. If you are sad, disappointed, envious, angry, excited, or ashamed, try to unearth these emotions and reflect on them. You are not a robot or a doormat. You have feelings, and that is simply part of the human condition. You are not here just to serve, labor, or provide. Homecoming is a decision to live fully, and a full life has a range of emotions.

Homecoming is not about what other people want, expect, or even demand that I feel. Neither is it about holding space for everyone else's tears while suppressing my own. Homecoming is about being honest with myself about what I feel. If you're not sure what you feel, tune into your body. Emotions can make themselves known through a racing heart, an upset stomach, a tightness in the chest, or warm cheeks. Some therapists say, "Get out of your head and drop down into your heart/body." This means connecting with your emotional and physical responses. Staying in your head can be a way of disconnecting from yourself; you can rationalize why you need to stay in a toxic environment while your body cries out to escape. You must learn to observe the early signs of fatigue, frustration, and fear. The rational mind is not more important than your heart, body, and spirit.

Some of us have been performing for so long that we have lost sight of the truth of how we feel. We want everyone to believe that everything is fine. We want to appear strong and flawless. These performances are exhausting and do not leave room for us. We need to find or create spaces where we can be at home with ourselves, with our thoughts and feelings. For some, that may be in the shower or alone in the car. Let's set the intention of carving out more space where we are free to feel and express what we feel.

Suppressed or ignored feelings can erupt in tearfulness, rage, teeth grinding, sweating, pacing, hair loss, binge eating, and even self-harming behaviors such as cutting. As we make room for truth, including the truth about what we feel, we become better able to express and regulate our emotions. Think about what you currently do to calm your nerves and consider whether the action actually leads to a perpetual state of running from yourself.

One reason why we run from our feelings is because acknowledging how we feel may require us to make some changes. If you told yourself the truth about how you feel about your job, your relationship, or your family, you might need to make some hard decisions. I invite you in this moment to acknowledge how you feel in your body when you are in the presence of your significant other or a family member, or at your workplace. As you raise your awareness, your consciousness, you move closer to home.

I invite you to consider some of the feelings associated with disconnection from self. Boredom often flies under the radar, but if you are bored, it usually means you are living beneath your potential. Perhaps you have been living on autopilot, following the path you started even if it no longer speaks to you. Are you living without passion or purpose? When you are checked out, you don't even notice when the joy left (if it was ever present). If you are honest with yourself and discover you are bored with your job, relationships, or spiritual path, this is a sign that it is time to come home to you. Homecoming is a decision to occupy your life, to engage with what animates you and breathes new life into the dry bones of your circumstances. Boredom does not always mean you need to exit! Your job or relationship may be boring, in part, because you stopped fully showing up. Neglected plants wither from lack of sun and water. Boredom is a sign that you need to check back into life and nurture the gifts within you and in your life. Some of you have financial circumstances that make you feel stuck in a career or a job that brings you no fulfillment. I would encourage you to consider ways to infuse joy or fulfillment into your day—both during and after work hours.

Another emotional sign that you need to come home to yourself is envy. When you judge yourself harshly for your feelings, you increase your difficulties; consider how envy is giving you information about your desires. If you are envious of other people who appear to have financial freedom, a loving relationship, a family who cares about them, children, a healthy body, or even confidence, it's important to not beat yourself up for wanting what you are lacking. The key is to turn your gaze inward and give yourself space to experience your feelings. You may have unresolved grief about the childhood you had or didn't have. You may be frustrated or disappointed about physical or psychological conditions that you have to live with. You may feel angry about the ways you have had to struggle financially. As you come home to yourself, you can acknowledge the feelings beneath your envy. By accepting what you can't change and acting on what you can, you manifest the life you want. If you envy confidence, work on building your confidence. If you envy a relationship, begin confronting barriers that may be in the way of your forming relationships. If you envy people with privilege who benefit from oppression, begin organizing and engaging with social justice.

Sometimes we are comparing our real lives to other people's social media lives, and there is often more to the story than people's photos of never-ending smiles and success. Finally, as you come home to yourself, you can acknowledge your unpleasant feelings about what you don't have while still being able to celebrate with your friends who have attained or have always had the things you desired. You can grieve your difficulties with infertility and still celebrate the birth of your friend's child. You can acknowledge your loneliness and longing for companionship while still authentically being happy for your friends who have found love. Emotions are complex and layered, and you can feel more than one thing at the same time. Accepting the complexity is a part of a psychological homecoming.

Another indicator of emotional disconnection is an inability to experience joy. When life is difficult, we can become hypervigilant, so when things are going poorly, we feel sadness, anger, and despair, but when things are going well, we wait for the other shoe to drop. When I am perpetually despairing, I am not at home with myself. As we experience homecoming, we can breathe, we can feel, and we can even enjoy the good. This is not easy, but I invite you to set the intention of feeling the full range of emotions, including joy. As we begin to invite joy into our lives, we can initiate the process of taking down the walls that have kept us from living in the present, especially when we face the vulnerability of enjoyment. I invite you to give yourself permission not to live in warrior mode, recognizing that you want more from life than survival. You can cultivate joy by spending time doing things that animate your life and by engaging with people who fill you with joy.

On the other end of the emotional spectrum is anger, and some of us have difficulty accessing it. You may have grown up in a home or community where children were not permitted to express negative emotions. The reality is that some things are outrageous, and when we cannot experience or express outrage, we often turn those feelings inward so that it manifests as depression. Related to anger is frustration, which we experience when we have a goal, desire, or need that is not met. When we are mistreated or disrespected, we may feel embarrassed, sad, or numb; we may also feel a block that makes anger inaccessible. For those who think all anger is unacceptable, consider that experiencing anger does not dictate what one does with the anger. True, destructive anger may lead us to destructive actions against ourselves or others, but constructive anger can motivate us to make change, to use our voice, and to recognize our agency. Some of the significant moments of progress in human history have resulted because people became outraged about injustice and then worked to turn things around. One way you can regulate your anger is to adopt a practice of scaling events. I have worked with clients on this to help them rate the severity of an infraction so that they can then determine an appropriate response. This is important for those who quickly escalate from 0 to 10 and explode over minor incidents. Consider the types of events that are mildly irritating and would get a score of 1 or 2, and go all the way up to 10, determining the types of events that are increasingly upsetting. Then you can go back and think about the options for a response to a minor irritant as opposed to a level 10 violation. Being able to respond appropriately to upsetting events is an important aspect of homecoming.

*Ellen, an Asian American woman in her fifties, lives with major depression and substance dependence that sometimes surfaces as irritability and angry outbursts. After a few months in therapy, she shared very matter-of-factly about the physical abuse that her father inflicted on her (without using the word abuse). I asked how she felt about her father's actions, and she responded, "It just happened. I don't feel anything. It's probably all my father knew." When I began naming the potential feelings she might have, she rejected the idea and changed the topic. Months later, she spontaneously shared how she felt during the abuse and how she feels about it now. We were then able to explore what feelings she was not permitted to feel or express as a child, and how she has since been quick to explode at any sign that a person may try to disrespect, dishonor, or hurt her. With fire in her eyes, she declared, "They better not try it." Connecting to her feelings, she created space to begin coming home to herself with truth.*

Yet another emotional indication that we are checked out of our lives is being stuck in resentment. There are likely ways in which we have been mistreated, devalued, ignored, neglected, or even abused. Unfortunately, in many cases, these experiences are not met with a just response. Often they were met with silence, and those who mistreated us seemed to get away with it. This can be very painful. We can feel incapable of moving forward when there was no closure, justice, or apology. It feels so unfair because it *is* unfair. However, when I am stuck in resentment, the offender continues to dictate my life. I am waiting for them to release me, and they likely never will. A part of homecoming is giving myself permission to take my healing out of the hands of those who harmed me. I open myself to the possibility that this person is no longer the center of my life. As you journey home to yourself, it will be helpful to continue to remind yourself that you are worthy of a full life, even if others did not treat you that way.

*Your tears are prayers.* Your sighs, tearfulness, aching body, and blank eyes often carry a story that you may not have had the words or freedom to express.

- Does the state of your life, internally or externally, fall short of what you imagined?
- Did you attain what you thought you wanted, only to discover that you still feel empty and unfulfilled?
- Do you have a sense of powerlessness or hopelessness?

- Do you lack the energy or motivation to pursue the things that used to matter to you?
- Do you feel there are no words to capture the ache in your heart?
- Do you find yourself crying often, or does it seem impossible to cry?

If you answered yes to the questions above, you may be facing depression, which for some is a sign of psychological homelessness. With depression, we can feel disconnected from others or even from life itself. I appreciate the effort you have taken to press through that storm cloud and begin this book. There is a lot of stigma surrounding depression, so your first instinct may be to reject the possibility that you have experienced it. Some aspects of depression may resonate with you, while others may not. It is important for you to recognize any sign that you are homesick or are missing yourself. Many of us have experienced symptoms of depression even when we did not know what to call it. Depression goes beyond sadness; by definition, depression disrupts our lives.

A part of your homecoming may require recognizing signs of depression and taking some steps back home to yourself. The reality is that reconnection to yourself may feel like you are meeting yourself for the first time. This is the case if depression or disconnection started early in your life.

Signs of depression include a depressed mood, difficulty sleeping (which may mean trouble falling or staying asleep or difficulty waking up), loss or increase of appetite, which may result in losing or gaining weight, a lack of pleasure in the things you used to enjoy, loss of energy, slow movement, a sense of hopelessness or the belief that things will never get better, and thoughts of self-harm or suicide.

For some people, depression shows up in nontraditional ways, such as high-functioning depression, irritability, or anger. Those with mild or moderate depression may be able to go to work each day, but the depression can become more evident after work when they are unable to move from the couch, immediately start drinking, or struggle with insomnia. If you find yourself barely getting through the day, breaking down when you're alone, or experiencing deeper anger, resentment, or a sense of being on edge compared to others or to your old self, you may be experiencing underlying depression. Depression is more than a bad day—it lasts at least two weeks and affects various aspects of your life. If you are living with depression, I would recommend psychotherapy, in addition to the following strategies to help you navigate the journey home.

1. Acknowledge the despair or depression and the circumstances that have created or contributed to your depression. We often judge ourselves harshly for our challenges without looking at the roots of the problem, whether related to biology, family, losses, oppression, or other forms of trauma.

2. Nourish yourself by spending time with people who affirm you, while reducing or eliminating time with people who make you feel worse about yourself.

3. Engage in self-care. If there are ways in which you have been neglecting yourself, a great way to begin this journey is to better attend to your needs (even if you have only enough energy for small steps). Have patience with yourself, tending to your hygiene, trying to eat healthy foods, and resting. Self-care is an important part of reconnecting with yourself.

4. Challenge negative thoughts. We want to be careful about the ways we think and speak about ourselves. When you experience shame-inducing thoughts, try to look for new ways to understand your experience. For example, you may say, "Although I have not had a loving relationship, I believe I deserve to be loved."

5. Help to improve your community. Sometimes we struggle with feelings of purposelessness. We can give meaning to life through

the impact we make on the world around us. Depending on the level of depression, engagement in this work may vary. Consider how you can support issues that are important to you—for example, the environment, antiracism, youth engagement, or gender equity. Recognizing what you care about can help you counter depression and raise your awareness of the issues that speak to you.

Another sign of emotional disconnection is anxiety and insecurity. Fear may be the trigger that pushed you to overextend yourself or caused you to be overly focused on what was happening around you in order to feel safe. Deep-seated fear may manifest as difficulty sleeping, headaches, nausea, trembling, difficulty focusing, restlessness, sweating, fatigue, guardedness, and overthinking. When you are frequently panicked, it can be difficult to come home to yourself.

One activity to ground yourself focuses your attention on the five senses and can help you to see yourself as a safe home base. When you panic, breathe intentionally and become aware of yourself and your surroundings, so you can regulate yourself and calm the panic. Let's practice now if that feels right for you. Look at the area around you and take notice of three things that you see. Then begin to pay attention to any sounds that you hear: a clock, an air conditioner, music or television in the background, someone else's voice, or the sound of your breathing. Notice if there is anything that you taste. You may have been chewing gum, drinking tea, or eating. Take a cleansing breath and notice the scents around you. You may smell cooking food, cleaner, lotion, perfume, or something unpleasant. Finally, become aware of what you feel on your skin. You may feel your clothes resting on your body, or you may feel the chair under you or the ground beneath your feet. Tune into the present moment instead of escaping to social media or drowning in the panic. Often, regrets and worries burden us and keep us disconnected from ourselves. Instead of being overwhelmed and activated by thoughts of the past or future, you can make the radical decision to occupy this present moment *fully*.

In addition to calming yourself through your senses, other activities can assist you when you are anxious or facing stress on your homecoming journey. Take time to sit still and breathe to reduce your anxiety. Other calming activities that can help you reconnect with yourself include trying aromatherapy, humming or listening to music, spending time with people who are a calming presence (co-regulation), reading sacred texts or self-help books like this one, drinking water or putting a cold washcloth on your face, enjoying self-massage, and setting boundaries so you spend less time with people or activities that contribute to your stress.

Perfectionism is also a sign of disconnection from our authentic selves. When we struggle with perfectionism, we prioritize our performance and productivity to the neglect of our inner lives and sometimes our physical bodies as well. Instead of feeling and knowing that we are enough even when we are still, we may feel the need to stay busy to compensate for shame and insecurity. Perfectionism can emerge from a desire to prove people wrong after they mistreated, abused, bullied, or ridiculed us. It can also result from harsh parenting, coaching, and teaching that praised perfection and competitiveness. Some of us were trained to believe that love, attention, respect, or care were conditional, based on our performance. Perfectionism can also emerge from the need to be independent very early in our lives because our parents may have struggled financially, physically, or emotionally. In addition, perfectionism can result from growing up in an environment where any moment of weakness or vulnerability could threaten our sense of safety, so we had to be vigilant at all times.

Coming home to yourself will require giving yourself grace. In mindfulness meditation, there is a principle called beginner's mind, which describes an openness to learning and growing, adopting a curiosity about the world within and around you rather than feeling the need to know it all. In Christian scripture, there is a teaching that says that in order to enter the spiritual realm of God, one must have the humility of a child. Essentially, the lesson for us is to stop fighting and clawing our way to status, self-justification, or a fragile sense of self-importance based on scorekeeping. Whether we call it beginner's mind or childlike humility, homecoming involves freeing ourselves from the pressure of perfectionism.

With homecoming, you will realize that you are enough. You are worthy. You can rest in the truth of that and embrace the learning journey. No script or costume is required here. You can show up for this journey home with your doubts, frustration, tears, scars, imperfections, and wonder. This journey is for you. No pressure. You do not need to race through the pages of this book. Read, reflect, and breathe. Find the parts that speak to you and allow yourself to hear with new ears and to consider news ways of showing up for yourself.

## HOMEWORK

For this chapter's homework, I encourage you to intentionally take time to reflect on and perhaps even share your feelings. Consider how you are feeling in this moment, in this season of your life. The answer may be layered and complicated. I invite you to allow for the complications and contradictions. You may feel one way about your relational life and a different way about your financial situation. You may feel one way about your current spirituality or religious faith but feel a different way about the state of your physical health and well-being. Try not to fall into the trap of allowing one emotion to silence the others. In order to begin communicating and regulating your emotions, consider journaling about them or sharing them with someone who asks how you are feeling. What will it be like to tell them the truth regardless of their response? Consider sharing simply for the sake of speaking the truth, so that your feelings are not dependent on a particular response. There can be liberation in speaking truth, even to ourselves.

I invite your soul to tell your heart, mind, body, and spirit, "Welcome home."

# CHAPTER THREE

# External Signs of Disconnection

*About twenty years ago, when I first graduated with my doctorate in psychology, I noticed a concerning pattern within myself. I was primarily working with trauma survivors, which is my area of expertise, and I was in charge of my appointment calendar. I found myself scheduling clients all day without a break. Initially I would have an hour for lunch, but inevitably, if I received a request for an appointment, I would schedule the person during my break. I even rationalized it to myself by saying, "What's more important? A sandwich or someone's healing? A slice of pizza or someone getting relief?" Of course, in framing it that way, I would skip the meal and see the person. One day I was working with a client and talking to them about the importance of taking care of themselves. As I was offering this heartfelt message, I noticed that my stomach started growling. What a contradiction! I had to have a meeting with myself and decide what kind of psychologist I wanted to be. Did I want to be a hypocrite and talk to people about valuing themselves while I simultaneously devalued myself? I did not want to just talk about wellness, I wanted to live it. I had to come home to myself. I began to do that by protecting*

*my time, my health, and my care. For me, homecoming sometimes*
*requires telling a client no so I can say yes to nourishing myself.*
*Coming home can also look like going for a walk or dancing in*
*the middle of the day. Sometimes it looks like taking a break be-*
*tween sessions to call a friend, stretch, make a cup of tea, or med-*
*itate. Coming home to myself is a daily decision and a soul-based*
*commitment. Authenticity is contagious, so as I ground myself in*
*authentic living, it lights the path for others I encounter on the*
*journey home.*

In this chapter, I will describe some experiences that may have caused you to lose sight of yourself. Then I will explore some of the external signs that may indicate a need for this homecoming journey. While the previous chapter focused on internal signs, namely emotions, this chapter will focus on external signs: behaviors, actions, or in some cases, inaction. Sometimes we say that we are comfortable and connected with ourselves, but our actions reveal a different reality. External signs may include but are not limited to addiction, emotional eating, staying in dead-end situations, settling, unhealthy relationships, and self-sabotage. As you read, I invite you to reflect on your journey and the ways your actions may be revealing a longing for home or a disconnection from yourself.

## THE SETUP:
## CIRCUMSTANCES THAT PREDATE YOUR ACTIONS

We often carry a lot of shame and/or guilt about actions we have taken at different times in our lives. We have engaged in some behaviors that we would rather not broadcast or publicize. If you have found yourself acting in destructive, conflictual, or unhealthy ways, aspects of your story can usually help you understand how you ended up in this pattern. Stress, trauma, and loss may have caused you to lose sight of yourself. Disappointment or betrayal may also have derailed your life's journey. For some, rejection by others led to rejecting yourself. Societal barriers to reconnecting with ourselves include poverty and discrimination, which can be sources of stress and trauma that cause us to shrink ourselves and prepare for the worst. Being the only person from your demographic or life experience can be stressful and demoralizing. You may face stigma, stereotype, barriers, hate, avoidance, and even professional or personal attacks that leave you doubting your abilities and feeling like a fraud (impostor syndrome) and thus lock you out of certain opportunities for promotion in addition to the locks put in place by systemic oppression. As a result, you may have buried yourself in your work, spent a lot of energy perpetually trying to prove others wrong, or become consumed by shame, anger, or depression. Living and working in places with pervasive oppression can require such vigilance that you overlook your needs and your care. Additionally, there may have been times when you stepped out of the shadows and risked showing up only to face disappointment, rejection, and closed doors. These painful experiences can cause us to withdraw from others and even from ourselves. Let's take a closer look at the stop signs that tell us to turn around and head home to ourselves.

## CONSTANTLY BEING BUSY: THE TREADMILL OF LIFE

*Beverly is a grieving mother whose young adult daughter died a year ago. Beverly approached her grief with the same strategy she used when she experienced childhood sexual abuse and sexual harassment: She kept busy. Beverly is successful in her career, but underpaid. She is a member of many community and religious organizations; she also is the founder and leader of her own nonprofit organization. COVID-19 was devastating for Beverly even though no one she knew died from it and she still had a job. It was devastating because for the first time in her life, she had to be still. COVID-19 pushed Beverly into her own homecoming journey. In the mandatory stillness, her grief exploded—both for her daughter and for her younger self. In the stillness, she encountered the pieces of her broken heart.*

Coming home to yourself requires slowing down. We have often mistaken being busy for being healed, but busy is not the same as healed. You may have received the message that doing a lot means you are worth a lot. In this way, productivity becomes a measure of a person's value. When insecurity and fear are the driving forces behind our actions, or when we have bought into capitalistic notions of self-worth, we can easily fill our days with activity while remaining disconnected from ourselves. The gift of homecoming is having a positive regard for your presence, your wellness, your life. You have nothing to prove to yourself. You can breathe. You can choose sacred stillness. You can rest. You can stop being controlled by the push of toxic culture and internal unhealed wounds. You can interrupt the constant rushing and the hustle and bustle of busywork—purposeless, frantic efforts to prove you are worthy. You begin to know in your bones that you are enough, and even when you don't fully believe it, you still give yourself breathing room to be, to heal, to feel, and to come home.

This message is especially relevant if you have faced discrimination—for example, if you are Middle Eastern, Jewish, trans, impoverished, undocumented, Black, Indigenous, or underrepresented in another way. If you have one of these identities, people likely told you that the key to dismantling oppression is to lean in, do more, show up and be more. It is problematic to shift the focus away from toppling systems of oppression and instead place the burden on oppressed people to try harder. Black people have been told from the inception of their forced arrival in the United States that their worth was based on their ability to labor and produce for other people's edification and consumption, all while denying their very humanity. Again, instead of dismantling racism, Black and Indigenous people and other people of color learn to strive to be twice as good, to work twice as hard, and to prove to others that they are worthy of respect, humanity, and a livable wage. Survivors of other forms of trauma also receive the message that they need to earn the approval of the very people who aren't committed to seeing them. To come home to yourself is to reject the pressure of self-erasure and perpetual busyness. You can tell yourself the truth: busyness has not brought healing or relief, only distraction and superficial accolades. You desire something much deeper and more fulfilling than a new job title and more liberating than the temporary favor of public opinion.

Busyness can also show up as perfectionism. When you disconnect from yourself, nothing you do is ever enough to bring fulfillment, peace, or self-approval. Consistently being ignored, overlooked, or rejected may have trained you to stay on the track of striving to be something you are not. With perfectionism, you become very hard on yourself and rarely, if ever, celebrate your successes. To come home to yourself is to choose the radical act of stillness. I sometimes refer to this as settling your spirit. This is getting to a place of inner peace that silences the anxiety that constantly demands your attention. To settle my spirit is deeper than choosing meditation or stillness as an obligation, a new trend, a tool, or even a badge of honor. To settle my spirit is to, at my core, turn off the comparison and competition and remind myself I am enough, just as I am.

## DYSFUNCTIONAL DISTRACTION

*Alo is a middle-aged, college-educated, married Native American father of three who is one of the few people of color at his job. White supervisors and coworkers have socially excluded him and passed over him for multiple promotions. His supervisors have consistently given him the tasks and responsibilities of*

*someone above his rank, but they have refused to give him the ti-*
*tle or salary increase. The stress of racism at work, including mi-*
*croaggressions by coworkers making offensive "jokes" about his*
*culture, has left Alo feeling frustrated and depressed. Over the*
*past few years he has increasingly turned to food for comfort and*
*distraction, and as a result, has gained eighty pounds and now*
*has several health challenges. Grieving the withheld opportuni-*
*ties for advancement, Alo has become silent and angry at work*
*and at home. He has disconnected from himself and others; Alo is*
*in need of a homecoming and an equitable workplace.*

Spending much of our time in toxic, dysfunctional, draining spaces can contribute to disconnection and emotional homelessness. If you have ever spent months or years of your life in an unhealthy relationship, home life, or toxic workplace, you will recall the ways in which that space took you out of yourself. In some ways, to survive those spaces, we have to disconnect from or retreat within ourselves, not letting those around us truly see us, as it is unsafe to reveal ourselves in those places. There are three primary types of coping, and each one in moderation can be helpful. Emotion-focused coping involves engaging in activities that help to soothe our hearts, such as talking to a friend or journaling. Problem-solving coping is doing something about the issue to resolve it. Finally, there is distraction coping. For those who are anxious or tend to overthink issues, distraction in moderation can be helpful so you do not become overwhelmed. However, sometimes we perpetually distract or numb ourselves to the point that we have actually abandoned ourselves.

I invite you to consider the ways you have sought to disconnect that have brought a level of dysfunction into your life. Numbing yourself to life is an indication of emotional homelessness. Some of us seek escape through constant sleep, but even when we awaken, the issues and hurt are still present, and this reality causes us to feel exhausted even after a full night of sleep. Like Alo, some of us medicate with emotional eating. Others seek escape through sexual intimacy, perpetually running from ourselves to the presence of another. If we are honest, though, there is a level of peace that we desire that cannot be attained through numerous desserts or orgasms. Can you acknowledge that you have eaten delicious meals that did not bring you home to yourself? Can you acknowledge that you have experienced physical pleasure that left a part of you still unfulfilled?

Rather than engaging in emotional eating when your body is actually not hungry, you may want to begin asking yourself, "What am I really hungry for?" Then examine and explore ways that you can address the true hunger, need, or point of dissatisfaction. The deeper craving is often at the level of the heart, mind, or spirit, but we shut down the message by stuffing ourselves. We stuff and silence our grief, anger, despair, and loneliness with food, alcohol, or other substances. Our distractions give us the illusion of fulfillment, but this does not last. When I release the weight of self-silencing and free myself to feel, express, and attend to my feelings, I often don't need to stuff myself. Our inner self is calling us to create a life we do not need to escape from or numb away. To end the distraction, let's begin to pay attention to the neglected parts of ourselves—our wounds, our dreams, our fears, our stress, and our hopes. Consider the parts of yourself that are longing for activation so you can be present to your life. Let me say clearly that the issue is emotional eating as a way of avoiding or numbing ourselves. This should in no way be used to justify fat shaming or sizeism (discrimination on the basis of a person's size).

Sometimes we justify numbing out by saying, "I just want to reward myself or give myself a treat." As I come home to myself, I begin to tell the truth about the poison that I have called a treat. The toxic habits and even relationships that I have turned to were actually destructive and dishonoring of myself. As I come home, I remove the blinders, and this increased awareness allows me to make more honest decisions to create an abundant, fulfilling life.

Not only might we seek to escape with sleep, food, drinking, drugs, and sex, but we might also turn to shopping, monitoring the lives of celebrities, and even gossiping about other people. One distraction technique many of us aren't cognizant of is the creation of drama. Some of us have become experts in chasing and creating drama, because if I have a lot going on out there, I do not have to confront what is happening here, within me. Some of us keep an argument going because confusion and conflict are familiar to us—these might have been part of our upbringing. We may mistakenly believe peace is boring, fake, or an indication that people do not care for us. If I am at peace with drama and uncomfortable with solitude, it is highly likely that I am disconnected from myself. If I am in warrior mode, fighting others all the time, I am likely missing my sense of home. I am unsettled and need everything around me to reflect my state of mind.

Whether we medicate ourselves with vodka or chocolate cake, whether we distract ourselves by judging others or perpetually staying busy, the reality is that we have been drifting further away from ourselves. We all have things we turn to that do not edify or truly heal us. Spiritual bypassing—the clinging to our identity as spiritual beings to the point of denying our human condition, hurts, or challenges—is another form of distancing and distracting. If I cannot bear to look at my life and my circumstances, but instead hide in spiritual slogans, I am also not at home with myself. Whether I named your strategy or not, I hope you have given thought to how you have routinely left yourself behind, so you can instead make the decision to show up for yourself in truth and compassion.

## UNHEALTHY RELATIONSHIPS

*Emily, a young Jewish woman, was working at her first full-time job when she began dating Lewis, one of her coworkers. This was her first "adult" relationship, and she was excited about it. Initially Emily thought Lewis's possessiveness and jealousy were compliments and positive signs of how much he liked her. Over time, his constant accusations that she was flirting and/or cheating, as well as the demands that she wear only clothes he selected, became stressful. She often found herself crying and pleading to gain his trust. Lewis also began demanding sexual acts that Emily was not comfortable with, and he would insult her body before, during, and after sex. When Emily broke down and told Lewis she wanted to break up, he threatened to kill himself if she ever left. This threat was reinforced when she met his parents and they told her how much they appreciated her being there for Lewis because he had been very depressed before he met her. Not long after he introduced her to his parents, Lewis's physically abusive behaviors escalated, leaving Emily hiding scars and bruises. Emily began missing work, avoiding family and friends, and sinking into a deep depression. One day she caught a glimpse of herself in the mirror and literally didn't recognize herself. This was her wake-up call. She needed a homecoming, and she knew she would need to get support to escape this abusive relationship.*

Another indication of homelessness or disconnection from self is being in relationships that dishonor you. Whether the abuse you experienced was emotional, verbal, sexual, or physical, you must acknowledge that being in that relationship made it impossible for you to authentically be at home within yourself because you were not affirmed, appreciated, respected, or cared for. When you've sought the affection of those who demean, reject, or ignore you, you've had to neglect yourself, to varying degrees, as that other person has also neglected you. You may have tried to make the relationship work out of fear, boredom, loneliness, insecurity, love, or hope that it would improve, but being in an unhealthy relationship weighs down your mind, heart, body, and spirit. When fear keeps you in a place destructive to your well-being, you often have to emotionally disconnect. The longer you're in the relationship, the more you disconnect from your heart and perhaps even your body. Disconnection or detachment as a survival strategy may feel like a superpower, and it may have allowed you to make it through the days, months, or even years. However, the more you are dishonored, humiliated, ignored, or abused, the greater the disconnection required. Mistreatment usually escalates over time, so what may have started as minor offenses can escalate to major assaults on your psyche. When we adjust to dysfunction, including dysfunctional relationships, the cost is high. We end up paying with our very beings, the essence of who we are.

Clearly, decisions to stay do not occur in a vacuum—the realities of violence, threats, manipulation, social pressures, and lack of resources can create barriers to escape. Some of us stayed because of insecurity, the familiarity of mistreatment, or even the moments of goodness that occasionally occurred in the relationship. Regardless of the internal and external factors that kept us in those draining relationships, we can acknowledge there was a cost—in the form of depression, anxiety, post-traumatic stress, and abandonment of self. Let us consider the times we abandoned ourselves in pursuit of the approval, validation, love, attention, or provision of another. When you are told that aspects of yourself are unacceptable or unlovable, you may try to reshape yourself in the likeness of someone else's ideals. Dealing with manipulative people can lead to silencing our voice in the hope of gaining or keeping what is presented to us as love. At times, we have fallen in love with someone's potential instead of who the person actually is. Authentic love requires that people have the freedom to show up as their authentic selves. Real love is rooted in truth, and truth is key to the homecoming journey.

It is my hope that you have the clarity, confidence, safety, resources, and support to never again become trapped in a relationship that undermines your worth, drains your spirit, or requires you to abandon yourself. I encourage you, going forward, to pay attention to how you feel in the presence of those who claim to care about you. Do you feel comfortable or uncomfortable, stressed or at ease, encouraged or discouraged, tense or free, like you're walking on eggshells or dancing freely? Our minds can sometimes convince us to ignore or minimize our concerns, so it is important to tune into your heart, body, and spirit. Living with an awareness of yourself can liberate you to tell yourself the truth even when the truth is about your need to release or escape unhealthy relationships. We can start this process with compassion for ourselves. Being in unhealthy relationships is draining and chips away at our self-confidence.

I invite you to consider that you can be worthy of something you have never received or experienced. Even if you have never been loved for who you are or without the contamination of fear, I invite you to consider that you are worthy of that. You are worthy of safety, respect, truth, and authentic love—and as you consider this, you may want to start with giving those things to yourself. As we heal the wounds that may have caused us to doubt ourselves, we begin to walk (or run) away from spaces and people that hold our voice, body, heart, mind, dreams, or safety hostage. The truth is that how you are treated is not a reflection of your worth or identity. You may believe or you have been told that if you deserved better, you would be treated better, but this is not true. To devalue and demean another person speaks to an issue with the abuser, not the abused.

You may have remained in the relationship due to religious pressure. I invite you to reexamine your faith or spiritual beliefs and to explore them in terms of your well-being and liberation. Often we are taught to erase ourselves in service of others. The reality is that you are a sacred being, and the foundation of most faith traditions is love. It is not about a world in which everyone else feels love while you feel desecrated and dismantled— that liberating faith should be applied to you as well. Look for the ways in which love shines back in your direction, not just at your ability to love those who seek to destroy your spirit.

Some of us stayed in an unhealthy relationship not because of insecurity but confidence. You believed you could change them. You believed your love would be enough. You believed your loyalty would be rewarded.

Your faith and effort could be strong enough to make them treat you right. But today you can make room for authentic love, a relationship and a partnership rather than a project or a rescue mission. I invite you to consider the fact that sometimes success is walking away from people who are destroying you. Stepping away from mistreatment is not a failure; it is a win. It means you are walking in faith toward what you cannot yet see but what you believe is important. Walking away from mistreatment means walking toward wellness, mutuality, respect, freedom, hope, and yes, love. Escaping unhealthy relationships means walking back toward yourself. Can you tell yourself the truth, that there have been times when you had goals for others that they didn't have for themselves, that you wanted them to be different from who they consistently chose to be? So today homecoming is about choosing to see what is, not just what we want, and living from a place of truth.

In the field of social psychology, there is a concept called *sunk cost*, meaning that the more time, effort, and resources you put into something or someone, the harder it is to walk away from or release it. Some of us stay in unhealthy relationships because it feels too late to start over. You may feel like you have already put so much into it, so you might as well stick it out. I invite you to consider not just what you have already sacrificed in the past, but also what you want for your future. I invite you to consider not just what you can tolerate or endure, but what you can enjoy and embrace. Homecoming is taking the pen into your hands and writing your next chapter.

I do not take lightly the fact that some of you are staying in an abusive relationship out of fear of the abuser. Researchers have found that violence usually escalates when the abused person tries to leave. For you, the issue may not be about what you want but what is safe. I encourage you to reach out to agencies in your area to help you explore and create a safety plan, including the possibility of escape. In the meantime, please remind yourself that you are more than what your abuser says about you, and you deserve better than abuse and manipulation.

Those who stay in unhealthy relationships due to fear of loneliness may cling to crumbs for fear that there is no feast waiting elsewhere. The truth is that many people are in relationships and are still lonely, unfulfilled, and even unloved. I cannot guarantee that you will meet someone down the road, but I can invite you to consider if the road you are on is fulfilling, loving, nourishing ground for your growth and wellness.

## PEOPLE PLEASING

*Asad, a young Middle Eastern American man, is an expert at making people happy. Most would call him charismatic. He was raised by parents who were very critical and rarely affirmed him. As a child, Asad studied both of his parents to figure out what interested them, because he discovered that when he talked about those things, they would give him time, attention, and a sense of respect. He applied this skill to his teachers as well and quickly became a favorite at school. Asad gives compliments freely, as he silently hungers for some words of kindness, but even when those words come, they are never enough. Asad's insecurity has created a void that seems unfillable. As an adult, he is charming in work settings and on dates, and popular among his friends. What most people do not realize, however, is that under the smiles, Asad is exhausted, insecure, and terribly lonely. He knows many people, but feels no one really knows him. He has brought happiness to many people, but fulfillment has always escaped him. Asad longs to come home to himself.*

Extreme people pleasing is another sign of disconnection from or abandonment of self. If you always attend to the needs of others to the neglect of your own, your soul is likely longing for a homecoming. If you've experienced abuse or had a parent living with addiction, people pleasing may have become a survival strategy. You had to learn how to anticipate the needs and wants of someone else as a way of protecting yourself from harm. You may have been raised to tiptoe in the presence of people who were so self-absorbed, there was little room for your voice, needs, or feelings. As a result, you may default to people-pleasing mode without any awareness or active intention. You may even live in that psychological space of constantly adjusting and contorting yourself to please others even when it hurts you. Neglecting your garden as you tend to everyone else's can result in a betrayal of your mental health, your dreams, and your potential.

It is easy to overlook the fact that people pleasing is a problem because self-erasure is often rewarded. Employers like the self-sacrificing worker. Religious and spiritual leaders warn against selfishness. Parents who give their all for their children are held up as the model. Partners who sacrifice their dreams for those of their significant other are considered ideal. Volunteers and donors who give all of their time, resources, and energy in service of others are honored and celebrated. Indeed, each of these acts may be noble to a degree. But I'd like to draw your attention in this moment not to what you give others, but to what you do to care for yourself. I also invite you to consider the motivation for your sacrifice. Is it really a choice, or do you feel you must perpetually erase yourself in order to be a good person? I also invite you to consider how you feel when you please others compared to when you do not. Are you left feeing unfulfilled or unworthy when you go out of your way to make someone else happy? If they are not pleased, does that mean you are not a good person?

Generosity, compassion, and at times sacrifice are important aspects of our humanity. However, I invite you to consider the reason and cost of perpetually pouring out to others without ever being refilled yourself. As you come home to yourself, you are able to selectively give of yourself from a place of authenticity, not of emotional emptiness in search of approval. Like Asad, you desire that people know more of you rather than simply appreciating the service or care you provide them. You desire to be seen as more than a script or a role, but to be known in the simple truth of who you are. You are a whole being, so much more than the echo of someone else's ego. You deserve space to feel, think, disagree, reimagine, and create. When you take up space and come out of the shadows of other people's agendas for your life, you give yourself permission to disappoint others, to displease others. When people have placed you in a narrow box, you must choose whether to stay in it to please them or to break out.

## CONTROL ISSUES

It is often easier for us to see other people's control issues than to see our own. You may wonder why some friendships or relationships ended, or why people avoid you or are not responsive to you. Control issues can be based in fear or in entitlement. If you have experienced neglect or abuse, you may fear moments when you are not in control, because in the past, your lack of control has resulted in some painful experiences. Others may have also blamed you for the mistreatment. As a result, you may try to control everything and everyone around you. You may lack trust or faith in others' abilities or decision-making, and this sabotages your relationships. It can create a vicious cycle in which your controlling ways cause people to emotionally disconnect from you, which triggers your fear of abandonment and leads to more controlling behaviors.

In psychology, the term *the parentified child* refers to children who are biologically or emotionally the eldest and who are called upon directly or indirectly to take care of the parent and the household responsibilities. You may have been your parent's confidant, protector, provider, or support system. You may have been responsible for raising your siblings. When you grow up with adult responsibilities on your shoulders, this can create a need for control. Everything was on you, so now as an adult, you may find it hard to let go, trust, open up, or allow others to think and do for themselves.

If your parents, partners, or bosses have been domineering, abusive, or controlling, you may have an unhealthy view of how things are supposed to be. In fact, you may not even recognize their behavior as abusive. You may believe that this is what good parenting, partnering, or leadership looks like. I invite you to consider how you and others felt when under that person's control. I also invite you to consider the possibility that love and respect can flourish in the absence of abuse and control. Love and respect are not based in fear, silencing, and shame.

Some people feel entitled to have control over others. You may have been taught with words or actions that controlling others is your right as a man or as a wealthy or White or educated person. You may not see it as control, but I invite you to reflect on the way you think about and treat others. You may simply feel you know what is best for people. Your beliefs or assumptions are often rooted in stereotypes and oppressive messages that have been promoted in education, the media, your family and peer circles, and even religious communities. These messages can show up in unconscious bias and even conscious bias. To come home to authentic living is to challenge and even dismantle the lies you have been taught, not only about yourself but also about others. The aim in homecoming is confidence, not arrogance. Confidence is about feeling competent, capable, and compassionate. In confidence, I have no need to trample on others to feel positive about myself. Arrogance, on the other hand, is the belief that one is better, wiser, and more important than others. It is the puffed-up performance seeking to hide insecurity. This is a false homecoming. An authentic homecoming is liberating not just for us, but also for others. Any liberation built on someone else's subjugation is not truly a liberation.

I know that some of you have had to carry a lot of responsibility because others did not step up. But I want to invite you to consider the ways you may participate in this pattern. If everyone in your family, job, church, and elsewhere piles work on you and you continue to do it, you perpetuate the imbalance. I invite you to consider saying no, stepping back from some things and teaching others how to do some of these tasks. When you step back, others will step up. Or some things may not get done, and that may be okay. You need to release some control, responsibilities, obligations, and pressures so you can have some rest, balance, and joy in your life.

## SELF-SABOTAGE

*Ericka, who is White and nonbinary, has had professional dreams for years, but the doors of opportunity have not opened. The delays have created insecurity and resentment. After a long journey, Ericka finally had the opportunity to interview for a dream position. Ericka arrived at the interview late, was hostile toward the interviewer, and spoke very negatively about the industry. Ericka then arrived at a therapy session a few days later in tears, unclear about how the dream had turned into a nightmare.*

The final sign that we are in need of a homecoming is self-sabotage. It is bad enough when others block our dreams, progress, and well-being, but if we are honest with ourselves, there have been times when we have stood in our own way. We may sabotage our dreams, health, and relationships for various reasons. Some of us were taught to devalue ourselves, and we have internalized those messages to the point that we have difficulty truly recognizing our gifts, skills, or value. Others sabotage themselves out of fear. To prevent disappointment or failure, we may not even try.

I invite you to reflect on the ways you may have contributed to or even orchestrated some of your setbacks. This reflection is not meant to shame you but to liberate you with the truth. The good news is that if you limited yourself, then you also have the power to begin living more fully. Although you couldn't control everything that happened to you, you have a pen in your hand and can write your next chapter. Choose carefully the thoughts, beliefs, words, intentions, and actions you write on this new page. We cannot delete what was written in the past, but we can learn from those chapters and turn the page as we write a life story guided by self-compassion and truth.

We also need to consider the reasons behind self-sabotage. We sabotage ourselves in part when we come to see ourselves through the eyes of those who demeaned us. What are the lies you have come to believe about yourself? What are the emotional and psychological walls created by the painful experiences of your life? The lies, armor, and walls may be blocking you from receiving love, making friends, and manifesting your dreams. Homecoming involves healing the wounds separating you from yourself. This healing will allow people to meet you, not just your defenses. Even if you are still healing and building your confidence, you can start by shifting your behavior. Become mindful of your actions and set the intention to align your actions with your healed self. With each action that affirms your worth, you take a step closer to home.

## HOMEWORK

I invite you to make a sacred agreement, a covenant with yourself that you will not leave yourself behind as you go forward in your career, your relationships, your life.

The homework for this chapter is an invitation to raising your awareness through monitoring yourself. Select one of the external signs you have observed in yourself and take notice of each time you do it. Consider how you feel right before, during, and after engaging in the behavior. For example, if you find yourself eating when you're not hungry, drinking more than feels healthy, buying items you cannot afford, or choosing to spend your downtime with people who take you further away from yourself, reflect in your mind or journal about these acts of disconnection. As you raise your awareness, you open the path to more options and possibilities for the journey home. Your awareness provides the opportunity to choose a new path, one that leads you back to your authentic self. To see yourself more clearly is *not* an invitation to shame. It is an invitation to acknowledge where you are and how you want to live.

I invite your soul to tell your heart, mind, body, and spirit, "Welcome home."

# PART TWO

Packing Light: What to Carry on the Journey Home

# CHAPTER FOUR

# Reparenting Yourself

M any of us are disconnected from ourselves because there are some things that we didn't have growing up, ways in which we were not fully nourished, affirmed, prepared, or seen as children. As adults, we recognize that parents are imperfect people and that they did the best they could, given their own capacity, wellness, mental health, knowledge, and resources. In some cases, they may have grown since they parented us, but the season of our childhood is gone. Reparenting yourself means recognizing what you lost or what you were not given as a child and beginning to give those things to yourself now.

You may feel sadness, anger, disappointment, confusion, frustration, and even shame about the ways in which your parents did not show up for you. You may experience despair because your mother, father, or other caretaker did not empower, validate, or affirm you. The reality is that we cannot physically go back in time, but we can have corrective, therapeutic, and transformative experiences that allow us to heal and no longer live from the place of the wounded child. Can you acknowledge today that some of what you carry was born of childhood wounds? You may have wounds of neglect, of not being protected, nourished, or nurtured. Your parents' absence or the harm they caused may have resulted from economic stress, addiction, unresolved wounds of their own, untreated mental ill-ness, or any number of other causes. Parental wounds can shape the way you see yourself, your expectations of others, and the way you treat yourself and show up in places.

The beautiful thing about the therapeutic process, spiritual practice, and even self-reflection is that we have the spiritual, psychological capacity to shift, heal, and transform by doing for ourselves what was not done for us. We can spend years being stuck, sad, and mad about what we did not get, but if we just remain in that place, we will never fully manifest the fullness of who we can be. Instead, while we give ourselves space to grieve and permission to be angry, disappointed, or sad, we also can make the decision to give ourselves what we never had.

As you reparent yourself, you facilitate the journey home. Yes, it would have been beautiful to have your physical and psychological needs met by those who birthed and/or raised you. Receiving love from your parents provides an important foundation, but even if you did not have that gift, you can choose to give yourself a new foundation now.

If we are honest, we recognize that our inner child has thrown temper tantrums because of old wounds. The wounded inner child can show up in tearfulness, rage, self-destructive behaviors, panic, or even people pleasing.

- What are the ways in which your wounded inner child shows up?
- How often is your wounded inner child showing up in your work life, your romantic relationships, or your friendships?
- How often has your wounded inner child been in control?

When you look at the state of your life and the ways in which it is a response to what you never received, I want you to know that while this may be a painful reality, it is not one of finality. Although there may have been moments growing up when the presence of a more engaged parent would have made a huge difference, and you recognize the pain of not get-ting that protection and nourishment, I invite you to consider the truth:

Even then, you were deserving of care and protection. You do not get a do-over of those years, but some things can change now, regardless of your age. Whether you are a teen, a young adult, a middle-aged adult, or a senior, I encourage you to reparent yourself so some things within you can shift and so you do not permanently live out of your wound.

*Jamillah is a highly successful Muslim American woman in her thirties. Intelligent and talented, she has always worked very hard. While her parents love her and her siblings, her mother and father's anxieties and untreated depression have greatly limited their lives and the ways they show up emotionally for their own children. Jamillah financially, emotionally, and spiritually supports her parents and siblings and is also a leader in her professional field. She has developed the capacity to make friends, while very rarely letting people get to know her intimately. When she is honest, she admits that she doesn't really know herself. She has had a few dating relationships, but they never got serious. Jamillah is very self-contained; some have called her controlling. As a child and adult, her experience with people is that they are unreliable, so she chooses to bet on herself instead. While this feels like the wisest decision, she is often tired, unfulfilled, and lonely.*

Parental neglect and mistreatment can leave us confused about our identity because we did not really have someone consistently affirming who we were. Our parents may have treated us as nothing more than just outgrowths of themselves, burdens, servants, or tools to gain a sense of power or worth. Along with causing challenges in our sense of identity or self-worth, neglectful parenting can also cause us to have relationship problems because no one modeled trust, open communication, and affirmation for us. You may have never seen or experienced healthy relationship reciprocity, constructive communication, or consistent care, and as a result, you may find it difficult to emotionally give or receive. You may have people tell you that you are emotionally unavailable or emotionally "too much." People may call you overly dependent or closed off. Both ends of that spectrum of emotional connectivity can result from the inner child wound of never feeling safe to open up to someone. As an adult, you may find that others want you to be more open and vulnerable in friendship, family life, or romantic partnership. Perhaps it's not that you are unwilling to open up but that you don't know how to open up. You may genuinely not understand what people are asking of you when they say that they want more of you, or conversely, that you are too intense for them. Some of you would love to be different, but you don't know how because the way that you are now has been locked in for so many years. You may believe that being emotionally restricted or emotionally explosive is your identity, instead of recognizing that your way of showing up is based in an inner child wound.

Parental wounds can also lead to destructive habits. Your core belief might be that if the people who birthed and raised you did not see your worth, you must be unlovable or unworthy of care. You may find it hard to believe that you are deserving of respect and compassion, so you have trouble trusting displays of kindness from others. You may try to sabotage the relationship, attack the person, or avoid them. You may punish yourself and withhold rest, care, joy, and even love from yourself. You may struggle with self-defeating thoughts, self-harming behaviors, and self-destructive patterns based on a childhood wound of low self-worth.

The pain of the inner child can keep us disconnected, shaming and blaming ourselves. To come home is to open ourselves to the hope of repair. The reparative work does not depend on your parents' apology or transformation. It does not require them to find you and nourish you. Although that would be wonderful, you no longer have to wait for them; you can choose you. I want to share the process of reparenting yourself, which is available to you today. You have the opportunity to give to yourself as an adult some things you did not receive as a child.

## REPARENTING WITH JOY

One way to reparent yourself is by creating opportunities and cultivating spaces for your joy to be unleashed, for your joy to come alive. Attentive, emotionally healthy parents who have the physical, psychological, and financial means to be fully present would have the capacity and motivation to learn about their children individually. Everyone is different, and what awakens joy in one child may not in another. So healthy, balanced parents attend to their child's interests so they can create opportunities for the child to be in places and with people that activate their joy. If you have a child who is excited about construction sites, you might stop by the fence at a building site so the child can have the joy of seeing construction equipment. You might buy the child construction site toys or look online for children's videos about construction. If the child enjoys dance, you may look for affordable dance classes, watch dance videos together, and even go to a dance concert.

Some of you may have sorrow, anger, or disappointment about the ways your interests were not cultivated or celebrated as a child. In the present, you can reparent yourself by investing time and energy in the things that bring you joy. Workaholics can reparent themselves by setting boundaries on their workday and spending the extra time doing a hobby. If your home was joyless, you may be uncomfortable with play and leisure. Risk the discomfort and let yourself adjust to the goodness of pleasure. On the other hand, some of you may have been raised by parents who never took care of their responsibilities and pursued only pleasure. In that case, you may associate enjoyment with being frivolous and wasteful. It is important to discover the middle ground. You can enjoy your life and still be a responsible person. Give yourself the gift of moderation. Additionally, some of you may have lost the capacity for joy, so even if someone invites you to share in their joy, you feel stuck, awkward, uncomfortable, and tense.

*Jin is an Asian American, married father of adult children. He was raised by a workaholic father who died early. Jin idealizes his father and has modeled his life after him. Now that Jin is a grandfather who has seen the emptiness of his constant work, he decided to come to therapy and set goals to learn how to have fun, enjoy time with his family, and know he is enough and has nothing to prove. We had to first acknowledge the things about his father that he honors as well as the things that he no longer wants to duplicate in his life. Jin was able to grieve both the loss of his father and the experiences his father never got to have, as well as the emotional experiences he would like to give himself. He also committed to modeling different behavior for his adult children and grandchildren. While his homecoming journey began with grief, despair, and fatigue, he is choosing the path of joy as he seeks to reconnect with the diminished parts of himself.*

If you are not sure what brings you joy, I encourage you this week to seek your joy and to be open to trying new things. Maybe you never had the luxury of joy because you had to work from an early age to support your family, or maybe you had to focus on protecting yourself and your siblings from abuse or addiction in your family of origin. When you live with constant worry, there is little room for joy.

You can commit to making joy a lifestyle, so that it is not just a rare occurrence. You do not have to wait until you're burned out or broken down before you pursue joy. Consider what it would mean to you to shape a life where your joy is a priority, where you live as if you are worthy and deserving of joy. You do not have to wait for a parent or a partner to introduce joy into your life. Joy is a gift you can give yourself by spending time engaged with the things that make you come alive.

## REPARENTING WITH STRUCTURE

Parents who are attentive and present will mindfully (intentionally) parent their children by creating a structure that gives children a sense of stability and guidance. When there is reliability, children do not have to feel so anxious. They know what to expect over the course of the day and over the course of the week. It's not a coincidence that trauma psychologists advise parents of children who have been exposed to trauma to give the child a routine to help stabilize them. Children will adjust to a clock when they know their bedtime, the general time of their meals, when they are expected to do their schoolwork, when they can play, and even when they are supposed to do chores. Children can relax into the routine of the house, knowing there are standards, rules, and guidelines. They know what is expected of them and what they can reliably expect from their caregivers. They don't have to worry if someone is going to feed them. They don't have to worry if and when their parent is coming home. They don't have to live with the unpredictable nature of an abusive, rage-filled parent or the dysregulation of a household where adults are constantly partying all night with strangers (or predatory relatives) coming in and out of their room at night. Children with a sense of stability have a foundation to safely explore the world and thrive.

*When I was in elementary school, a mentally ill lady from our church kidnapped me from my school. I remember sitting in my classroom, and someone from the front office came and asked me if I knew Ms. Laura. Of course I knew her. She lied and told the front office my parents had sent her to pick me up. When it was clear I knew her, they let her take me. I'm blessed to say that before the day ended, I was rescued. My parents drove around looking for me after they learned I had been taken. They found me walking down the street, holding Ms. Laura's hand. I did not realize the danger I was in until I had already been found. (Many parents make the mistake of only telling children to beware of strangers, without recognizing that those most likely to harm children are actually acquaintances.) As you can imagine, after that day I became much more vigilant and distrustful. A part of my homecoming was learning to breathe and trust, both myself and others.*

As a psychologist, I have had clients who were placed in harm's way and no one rescued them. I remember one survivor of sex trafficking who asked painfully, "Why didn't my family come and get me? They knew where I was. Why didn't they come?" Even though parents cannot protect us from everything, engaged parents make their children feel like a priority. They give them a sense of being important and worthy of care, and one of the ways they communicate their care is with some level of structure or dependability.

If you want to reparent yourself in the present, consider the ways in which your life feels out of order or lacking in structure. The present moment is a good time to commit to:

- Establishing a sleep routine (going to bed at a certain time)
- Planning nutritious meals
- Rescuing yourself or seeking help when you have lost sight of yourself
- Regularly decluttering your life, emotionally and physically

What's the trash you need to take out if you are going to parent yourself? What in your life is creating stench? Can you commit to not making yourself comfortable in rotten situations, jobs, and relationships?

Consider the guidelines you need to establish to protect your bedtime, your time to rest. Reparent yourself and put the phone away so you can get some sleep. If you are going to reparent yourself, that means you are no longer getting all your meals from vending machines or drive-through windows. If you're going to reparent yourself, you need to put some greens on that plate! As you reparent yourself, give yourself more water to drink instead of nonstop soda or coffee. Reparent yourself and dress for the weather, remembering to grab a sweater, scarf, and hat. Reparent yourself and take your vitamins. Reparent yourself and turn the TV off so you can go read a book or go for a walk. Reparent yourself and set a regular schedule for your laundry, get rid of things you've outgrown, and make an appointment for a medical checkup.

Structure means not only routine but also boundaries. Some of you may wish that when you were a teenager, a parent had intervened in certain dating situations to say, "No, you can't go with them," or "No, you cannot take my child there." It would have been nice if someone had set a boundary to protect you physically, emotionally, or both. Now you are an adult, so consider these questions as you reparent yourself:

- What are the boundaries you need to set?
- Who are the people you need to reduce or eliminate time with?
- Where are the spaces you need to advocate for yourself more?
- What are your deal breakers at work and in friendship? Is there anything that is unacceptable to you? If not, why not?

You are worthy of care and protection. You deserve goodness and kindness. You can set limits to protect your time, energy, mental health, physical health, resources, and spirit. I know in terms of culture and gender, you may have been raised not to have any boundaries; but you may want to consider being an advocate for yourself, a protector of your emotional wellness, and even the parent you never had. So who are the people you need to stop entertaining? Can the mother, father, grandparent, elder in you arise and say that some people can't come into your home anymore? Can you allow your inner parent to speak and declare to those who are breaking your spirit, "Absolutely not. This is unacceptable."

To create some order, you need to make some decisions to clear out your life in the ways that a responsible parent would. In addition to reparenting yourself by cultivating joy and establishing structure, give yourself space to feel what you feel.

## REPARENTING BY HOLDING EMOTIONAL SPACE

*Abha is a twenty-three-year-old single South Asian American woman who was raised by an anxious father and a mother who is a workaholic. Throughout her childhood she tried to calm her father and please her mother. By the time she turned nineteen, she was tired of both of them. She became very isolated from family and friends. She returns her friends' calls only when she is feeling happy and energetic, which is not often. With dating partners, she tries to hold her emotions in because she is afraid of being too much emotionally, which she fears would lead to her being rejected or being a burden, as she experiences with her father. For Abha's homecoming, we had to create space for her to acknowledge and express her feelings without judgment or fear. As she became more honest with herself, she became more honest with her family and friends. Not everyone was comfortable with her new level of self-expression, but she felt good about coming home to herself.*

To reparent yourself, you need to create space for your emotions and teach yourself how to manage them. Your emotional well-being is important. Consider what your parents taught you about your feelings with their words, their treatment of you, and the example they set. Some of us learned negative or unhealthy habits from watching parents who did not have the full capacity or motivation to parent with emotional stability. If, while you were growing up, your parent threw things when they were mad, then as an adult you may still throw things and not think it's a big deal. If your parent expressed disappointment by cussing somebody out, then as an adult, you may still have difficulty imagining any other options. You may actually say, "I didn't have a choice. They pushed my buttons." Some of us are in our fifties and still threatening to fight people who don't do things our way.

In addition to seeing unhealthy models, you may have been given unhealthy messages. You may have been told not to be soft, emotional, weak, sad, upset, or anything other than grateful. You may have never seen someone model how to express, manage, or regulate their emotions. This is the season for you to reparent yourself and know that it is healthy to have emotions and to be able to feel them and express them without drowning or exploding. As you reparent yourself, you can decide that your feelings don't give you permission to mistreat people, even if they are your children or your partner. As I reparent myself, I give myself space to feel and express my feelings in nondestructive ways. I teach myself to use my words. I teach myself to pay attention to the way my body responds in certain situations, so I can honor what I feel and make decisions that align with my wellness.

You can decide to live differently from the examples that you saw growing up. If growing up, you felt like nobody cared how you felt, you can decide to give yourself space to feel what you feel.

## REPARENTING WITH ACCOUNTABILITY

Reparenting means you develop the capacity to check yourself, to correct yourself even if no one ever did. You may have been given the message growing up that you can act any way you want, that it doesn't matter how you treat people. As you reparent yourself, you can begin to recognize when you are out of bounds and even emotionally abusive toward others. You can begin to correct yourself and recognize when you have gone too far, or better yet, recognize when you're about to go too far and interrupt the pattern by making a new choice to calm yourself and express yourself. You can begin to reparent by intentionally demonstrating respect for yourself and others in the way you handle your emotions.

Healthy parents talk to their children about taking responsibility and apologizing for misdeeds. Healthy parents will also acknowledge and apologize when they are wrong or have made a mistake. As you reparent yourself, consider that you still need to forgive yourself for certain things. Also consider if there are people you need to apologize to. You may be an adult and still can't apologize because you never saw it modeled, so you associate apologies with weakness. If you avoid apologies, assume time will heal all wounds, and never take responsibility for your actions, your relationships will suffer from unaddressed ruptures. Being able to own your part in a problem is an act of growth and development. Accountability is necessary for reconnection with yourself. If you cannot see your issues and address them, you will remain disconnected from yourself in significant ways. As you reparent yourself, become intentional about being self-reflective and teachable. Learning is a lifelong process, and we don't have to pretend to be perfect or all-knowing. We can give ourselves grace and compassion, but that must start with truth-telling and a change in thinking and behavior.

*Juan is a forty-one-year-old married Latino man who grew up being the man of the house because his father was absent. He was used to being catered to in his home, as well as out in the community due to his looks, charm, and generosity. He came to therapy after being caught having an affair. He is Catholic and shared numerous biblical reasons why his wife needed to get over it so they could move on. As he shared, it became clear that his father was a married man who'd had an affair with his mother. It also became clear that every man he knew was unfaithful to his wife. Only by asking questions did I discover that Juan had yet to apologize to his wife. He initially denied the affair. When it became clear that his wife had evidence, he told her that he loved her and that they needed to protect their family for their children and because of their vows to God. Juan's wife did not say very much to him, but it was clear from his descriptions that she was emotionally withdrawing from the marriage. Juan needed to actually sit with his actions and the impact they had on him, his wife, his children, and the other woman. He had to develop a capacity for accountability, not only in the form of an apology but also in a determination if he even wanted to change his behavior. Before he could emotionally come home to his family, he needed to come home to himself with honesty and accountability.*

## REPARENTING WITH A SCRIPT FOR SELF-CARE

Some of us grew up taking care of parents and/or siblings and were directly or indirectly taught to neglect ourselves. When you reparent yourself, you throw away that old script that says you are unimportant, or that your needs are insignificant. You can write a new script that recognizes your value; you can begin taking steps to care for, nourish, and nurture yourself daily. If kids don't have someone to say no to them, many of them will watch cartoons and play video games all day and binge on junk food. What they take in affects what they put out, so if they consume too much junk, their attention span will be limited, and so will their energy level. As you reparent yourself, recognize that you don't want your mind, body, heart, and spirit to be full of junk. As you reparent yourself, guard what you watch and what you listen to. Also guard what (and who) you put in your body. Your food affects your mood. Your entertainment choices influence your thinking and life choices.

Be the kind of parent who is responsible and intentional about what you are exposed to. Be mindful of what you feed your spirit, what conversations you enter and exit, and what spaces you spend most of your time in. When you care about yourself, you are thoughtful about what you participate in. As you journey home, you will become protective of yourself and see yourself as a treasure who is worthy of goodness. You may need to revise the script you received from your parents about who you are and how you deserve to be treated. As you reparent yourself, you commit to taking better care of yourself holistically, mind, body, heart, and spirit. I invite you to rip up the script that says your thoughts, health, feelings, and spirit don't matter. Write a love letter to yourself, because your wellness is worth preserving.

*Alice, a Black American woman, was the oldest of seven and spent her childhood taking care of her siblings and her mother, who was chronically ill. As an adult, Alice poured herself into being a great wife and mother, which left little room for herself. Her home was always immaculate and could easily be featured in a home design magazine. On the surface, all was well. Beneath the surface, however, Alice was struggling. She had high blood pressure and panic attacks, and she struggled with obesity. It took years for the awakening, but Alice's physical and mental health challenges prompted her to try therapy, as she realized she needed to take better care of herself. Along with exercises that looked at her thoughts, feelings, and behaviors, we also took a womanist psychology approach to examine the messages she had received about the ideal woman, particularly the ideal Black woman, who is often presented as a self-sacrificing martyr. Once Alice's consciousness about these scripts had been raised, she was empowered to write a new script for herself that did not require her to erase, deny, or minimize her needs and value.*

## REPARENTING WITH LOVE

Caring parenting is rooted in love, not performance. Love is not dependent on perfect grades or perfect behavior; even when children mess up, caring parents continue to love them. Parents may get upset or disappointed by a child's behavior, but fundamentally healthy parents love their children. To reparent yourself requires developing and nourishing self-love. I invite you to *choose* to love yourself unconditionally. I invite you to *choose* to love yourself when you're doing your best and when you feel your worst. Reparenting based in love is not sometimes or fair-weather only. When the internal storms rage and you're disappointed, angry, or embarrassed with yourself, allow there to be love present regardless.

Healthy and loving parents will not say certain things to a child or about a child, nor will they act in certain ways, because those actions are counter to love. Likewise, as you reparent yourself, be mindful of the way you speak to yourself and about yourself. Be mindful of how you treat yourself.

Consider the things you will not do again because you love yourself too much. Consider the things you will start doing as a demonstration, an outgrowth of your love. As you reparent yourself, you begin to recognize self-harming, self-sabotaging behaviors and replace them with self-affirming, self-loving behaviors. In a famous Bible passage, 1 Corinthians 13, love is described by a number of attributes, some of which are listed below. Consider the ways you can live them out in your treatment of yourself:

- Patient
- Kind
- Honest
- Protective
- Trusting

- Hopeful
- Persevering

To reparent yourself, be patient with your progress, set a gentle pace for your life, and tell yourself the truth. As you reparent yourself with love, take steps to advocate for your physical and emotional well-being, believe in yourself, be hopeful about your future, and do not give up on yourself. Reparent yourself by affirming your value and making decisions that align with the truth of you who are. You can love yourself by pursuing opportunities for your healing and growth. When it is in your power, love yourself enough to deny access to people detrimental to your development. Do not align with people, activities, or attitudes harmful to your well-being.

*Donald, a thirty-five-year-old Black man, despised himself. He was physically abused as a child by his mother and sexually abused by a teenager in his neighborhood. As an adult, he had many failed relationships as a result of self-sabotaging behaviors. He was promoted at work several times due to his skills and intelligence, but he would eventually come into conflict with a manager or coworker and would sooner or later be demoted or terminated. Donald came to therapy the way he comes into other social settings, prepared to entertain. He came in with jokes and dramatic stories delivered with the precision of stories that had been told many times before. In the middle of one of his therapy performances, I interrupted him and told him that I thought it must be exhausting being him. By having his fatigue named, he could acknowledge it. I told him he didn't have to entertain me. I told him this space was for him to be able to breathe and heal. We began to unearth all the reasons he had difficulty loving himself and the costs he had paid over the course of his life for the lack of love. As the insight grew, his self-compassion also grew, and week by week he began coming home to himself.*

## HOMEWORK

-------------------------------------------------------------------

I invite you to journal about the things you want your inner self to know you need emotionally, physically, socially, materially, and spiritually, so you can reparent yourself. Reflect on and include the things that you want your wounded self to know about who you are. Then describe what it will mean to be authentic and consistent in how you think, speak, and act toward yourself. Consider how you will actively work to repair long-term wounds by intentionally nourishing yourself. On this journey home, commit to mothering, fathering, parenting, and nurturing yourself.

I invite you to place your hands over your heart or abdomen and advise your soul to tell your heart, mind, body, and spirit, "Welcome home."

# CHAPTER FIVE

# Emotional Intelligence

A common response to the question "How are you?" is "Fine, how are you?" But I grew up using a different script in church. When people ask, "How are you?" many would respond by saying, "Blessed." If they're feeling enthusiastic, they may even say, "Better than blessed," or "Blessed and highly favored!" While affirmations can be inspiring and positive, psychologists have found two important truths that should be considered here. First, it is possible to feel more than one emotion at the same time. Someone may feel blessed and also depressed or anxious, for example, but not feel free to express the unpleasant emotions in particular settings. Second, if we say an affirmation that we do not fully believe, it can create more stress. So if I know that I'm supposed to say I'm blessed, but I'm not feeling particularly blessed at that moment, the statement can create distress or even guilt and shame. Growing up with scripts, whether cultural or religious, can at times cause us to disconnect from ourselves. If you did not feel entitled to speak the truth about your feelings or even to acknowledge those feelings to yourself, emotional intelligence will be an important skill for the journey home to yourself.

Emotional intelligence is the capacity to be tuned into and to regulate your feelings, and to relate to others in a way that takes into consideration their emotional experience as well as your own. When you have disconnected from your feelings and other aspects of yourself, it is important to begin cultivating your emotional intelligence. Some of you may feel overcome by your emotions, and this sense of being dysregulated can at times be burdensome. You may feel things very deeply, and as a result, may have been labeled by yourself or others as "too sensitive." Emotions and the ability to access them can be a gift, but if they are challenging to contain or manage, you may want to work on acknowledging and feeling your emotions without being overwhelmed by them. Others may be unable to access or express their feelings—they may want to cry but the tears won't come, or they may believe a situation is worthy of grief or anger but can't feel anything. Whether you typically feel flooded by emotions or numb to them, emotional intelligence is a good skill to develop as you seek to reconnect with yourself.

Your internal world may at times become emotionally flooded or emotionally frozen. These challenges may have affected your relationships. You may have difficulty connecting to others, expressing yourself, or understanding the emotional reactions of others. As we journey home, it is vital to increase our awareness of our emotional experience and to successfully navigate the world of relationships, whether with colleagues, friends, a romantic partner, or family. Emotional intelligence can be an important focus for growth for all of us as we seek to live authentically and compassionately within ourselves and in relationship with others.

## WHY IS EMOTIONAL INTELLIGENCE IMPORTANT?

*Adriana, an Afro Latina in her thirties, is the oldest of four children. A major source of pain in her life is her relationship with her mother. Her mother loves her, but the way she demonstrates this is by offering unsolicited advice and constant criticism. Her mother's lack of affection pushes Adriana away, and Adriana's distance leads her mother to conclude that Adriana has never liked her. This cycle has resulted in years of disconnection, although they both desire connection. Adriana and her mother need support to learn how to connect with their feelings and to communicate their feelings to each other. They need to come home to themselves individually to create the emotional space to be at home in each other's presence.*

Each of us can benefit from:

1. Becoming more conscious of our emotional state
2. Becoming more skilled in regulating our emotions so we don't go from withdrawn to explosive
3. Becoming better equipped to communicate our emotions and our emotional needs
4. Becoming more attuned to the emotional lives of others
5. Becoming more capable of effective engagement with people around emotional topics

These skills are part of emotional intelligence, and without them, we are often unaware of ourselves and others. This lack of sensitivity can cause us to act in confusing, harmful, or disturbing ways. Emotional intelligence allows you to be authentic with yourself and others, so you are not always following a script that doesn't necessarily match your circumstances. It allows you to tap in, honor the truth of the moment, and let down the barriers that would otherwise make you seem emotionally unavailable or unresponsive to people.

You may have spent a season sleepwalking through your life by being emotionally checked out of your personal relationships or work environment. Emotional intelligence can allow you to awaken and show up for yourself and others, rather than letting life pass you by.

## EMOTIONAL SELF-AWARENESS

*Dennis is a thirty-six-year-old White married bus driver who came to see me with many complaints about his wife. The list was endless, and the hostility was thick. He complained about her conversation, her parenting, her work habits, her ignorance about world events, her disinterest in sexual intimacy, and her appearance. The emotion he was comfortable expressing was anger, even outrage. After hearing him out for a few sessions, I asked Dennis to tell me about his fear. He looked startled and said, "What fear?" I took a breath and said, "I think you feel insecure and are afraid of losing your wife, who is very successful and whom you fear will not be satisfied with you." His eyes opened wide, and then he began to cry. He said, "Yes, I'm insecure. What can I do?" We had to get to the truth of his emotions in order to address the real issues within him and in his marriage.*

Your emotional self-awareness is your ability to recognize how you feel. This may sound simple, but often we are on autopilot with busy and distracted lives. In this era, we are often continuously on devices from the moment we wake up to the moment we fall asleep—watching television, making calls, joining video conferences, listening to music, and consuming social media, all of which leaves little time for self-reflection. With all of these devices competing for your attention, you have chosen to slow down to read this book. Being able to come home to yourself is essentially about being willing to honestly and compassionately sit with yourself and your thoughts, feelings, dreams, wounds, and memories.

In addition to all the distractions, we also face judgments that can keep us from recognizing how we actually feel. From when we are born, other people give us messages about how we should respond to our joy and our pain. We face countless expectations, demands, and pressures to act in a way acceptable to others, and this can require us to mute our hearts and our real feelings. Homecoming gives us permission to remove the judgment, censorship, and demands so we can actually express what we feel.

Let's take an inventory right now. If you release the idea that there is only one right answer and the fear that you will be a burden to others, how do you feel? How are you feeling about yourself, your career, your relationships, your past, and even your future? This question may feel overwhelming, especially if you haven't checked in with yourself in a while. You may have grown up in a family that taught you not to get caught up in your feelings, just to do what needs to be done. But at this point, honestly assess how you are feeling in your heart, mind, body, and spirit. Some of us never learned the full range of emotions and are limited to happy, sad, or mad. You may also feel fear, disgust, jealousy, interest, grief, surprise, joy, or distrust. When you feel these emotions, you may also experience bodily sensations. You may experience a change in your bodily temperature, you might start sweating, or you may feel an ache or pain in your chest or the pit of your stomach. Begin to give yourself permission to experience a range of emotions and to honor yourself by acknowledging the truth of what you feel.

When you are not aware of the reality that you can feel more than one emotion at the same time, you may ignore or deny aspects of your experience. I invite you to reflect now on times when you may have experienced seemingly contradictory emotions. You may feel loved and bored, or you may feel both grief over your losses and gratitude for what remains. We need to tell ourselves the truth about how we're feeling, because when we don't, then our actions, conversations, and decisions are a mystery to us. If you often find yourself thinking, "I don't know why I did that," or "I don't know what's wrong with me," then we need to take a sacred pause and truly reflect. Undoubtedly there is a reason, one often derived from unacknowledged emotions. When you have clarity about your feelings, your actions will usually make more sense to you. Instead of limiting yourself to only one acceptable emotion or claiming numbness, begin to dig beneath the surface of your response to see the root of your emotions. The truth may be that you are grieving, panicking, or even attracted to someone or something beyond your awareness. When you can acknowledge feeling intimidated, anxious, or even jealous, then you can address the real issue instead of running or becoming aggressive or ashamed.

I invite you to ask yourself questions about your emotions, especially when you feel bored or rejected. People with a long history of trauma have had to adjust to a highly intense environment. They may label an absence of drama or peace as boring, causing them to seek out drama. Those who often feel rejected may have an underlying insecurity that causes them to improperly interpret people's actions as rejection. For example, if someone doesn't text or call you back right away and you already feel insecure, you may interpret the delayed response as a rejection of you, when in fact the person may be working, sleeping, or going through an emotionally difficult time. Becoming more aware of what you feel will ensure that you don't make a mountain out of a molehill.

We are complicated beings, and in any moment, we can have layers of responses and reactions based on both our history and the current circumstances. Homecoming is about digging deeper into the truth of our emotions without judgment. You feel what you feel. What you choose to do about those feelings is another story. In other words, if you're bored with your job or your relationship, acknowledge that to yourself. Then you can begin to explore how to address that boredom. This self-awareness is especially important if you, like me, have had moments when you know your emotional response did not match the situation. If you sob uncontrollably in response to something minimal or if a minor offense leads you to explosive anger, there is more to the story. We need to attend to the unhealed wound, the distorted thought, or even the core belief we hold about ourselves to get at the emotional root that has been unearthed in the moment. If, for example, you fear that you are unlovable and you go on a first date with a person who never calls back, the grief and despair you feel are not really a response to this situation but to the larger fear of a lifetime of loneliness.

People can also become triggered by reminders of past traumatic events, as was the case for Joseph, a single, successful Asian American man in his fifties. When he was a teenager, an older man sexually assaulted him in a park right after it rained. To this day, the smell of wet grass makes him feel anxious and sad. His mind made an association that is difficult but not impossible to shift. Recognizing the negative association between the scent and the violation laid the groundwork for his homecoming, which involved disconnecting the trigger, the smell of grass, from the memory of violation, and connecting the scent instead to a range of experiences.

I invite you to consider people, places, and things that elicit an emotional response from you, whether painful or enjoyable. If you see a certain person, or even someone who looks like them, you may feel afraid, excited, amused, or angry. If a person behaves in a certain way, you may distrust them based on past unrelated experiences. You may also have associations with certain scents, foods, or streets. Your journey home is enhanced when you begin to notice your emotions and their causes.

Those of you who were taught that emotions were only a hindrance to logic and reason may wonder why it's so important to pay attention to them. Connecting with your emotions allows you to live as a full human being who's not cut off from parts of yourself. Embracing and learning from your emotions allows you to understand yourself better. Self-knowledge is the path to authentic living, and authenticity is necessary for homecoming. Discovering if you miss a specific person or if you simply miss companionship makes a world of difference. Discovering if you love the work you do or simply the amount it pays makes a difference in shaping the life you want. You may choose to stay in that relationship or that job regardless, but knowing your motivation and emotional investment frees you to choose from a place of honesty. As you learn what is truly going on within you, you will feel the liberation that comes from honoring yourself by living in alignment with truth.

## EMOTIONAL EXPRESSION AND REGULATION

*Stephanie is a forty-eight-year-old single African American woman who has many acquaintances but very few friends. Many people in her circle rely on her emotionally. She came to therapy with fatigue and resentment about how much she pours into others and how very little comes back to her. As we began to explore her friendships, we discovered that she rarely shares her feelings with her friends or dating partners. She assumes that her sharing would be an unwanted burden to friends who have their own stress, or that talking with them would not be helpful. In other words, she silences her feelings and needs and then is disturbed by her numerous one-sided friendships. I pointed out to her that when we always present ourselves as having it all together, people assume we actually do and it never occurs to them to offer support and encouragement. Mutual care or reciprocity requires a level of emotional communication that many find uncomfortable and risky, especially Black women and other women of color, who are often raised with the cultural values of self-sacrifice and service to others. This silencing, however, leaves many with unmet needs and unexpressed pain.*

Emotional intelligence is not only about recognizing what you feel, but also about learning to express and regulate those feelings so that you can be at home with the emotions without drowning in them. Expressing and regulating your feelings is not about silencing and censoring them for the sake of being controlling, but about preventing those moments that most of us have experienced when we acted in a way that was harmful to ourselves and others.

Instead of judging or distracting yourself, imagine sharing with others what you are feeling. A common phrase used to intervene with children who are having a tantrum is *Use your words.* Like the child who is lying on the floor, kicking and sobbing, we have had moments in our lives when words escape us. In those moments, we can feel the thickness of the pain, despair, or hurt, but we may be out of practice or too embarrassed to say what we feel. Learning to speak the truth of our feelings is a skill that can be developed over time. Consider how you usually act when you have a particular emotion, especially when those actions are not accompanied by direct communication. When you're afraid of being abandoned, do you abandon relationships prematurely? When you are angry, do you give someone the silent treatment and never discuss the issue? When you feel rejected, do you offer gifts, hoping someone will value you? When you feel insecure about your position at work, do you become irritable and controlling with your coworkers? Communication can make us feel vulnerable, and many of us did not see healthy forms of communication modeled. You may have seen silence, aggression, substance abuse, or religious engagement take the place of actual honest dialogue, but you have the capacity to make a different choice. You can begin to reclaim your voice and your emotional life by initiating and staying present in discussions about your feelings.

When you begin to express your emotions, you may feel panic. You may wonder if others will judge, reject, or manipulate you. These fears can cause you to retreat, shut down, or deny your feelings. This fear and discomfort are among the growing pains of coming home to yourself. Instead of going back to old patterns of suppressing your feelings and remaining silent, try the following strategies to stay engaged and present.

- Before you share, prepare yourself for the diverse responses the person may have. Sometimes we assume that people will react a certain way, and we are devastated when they go off script.

- Honor yourself with the reminder that your feelings are *yours* and are not dependent on others' response or agreement.

- Consider what you want to share even if it gets hard or you become anxious. You may want to write down a few notes or journal before sharing your feelings. Some of you may want to role-play or practice with a therapist or friend first. The more you share your feelings, the easier it becomes. Emotional expression may take practice, especially if you are used to remaining silent.

- Prepare by being thoughtful about the time and place where you initiate the dialogue. Some conversations are better had in private, while other times you may feel the need to have one other neutral or trustworthy person present to maintain a certain level of safety. Timing is important as well, because if you choose to share your deepest emotions when the other person is about to go to sleep or leave for work, you are likely not going to be heard.

- Remind yourself to breathe while you are sharing. Rest your hand on your belly or chest as a physical reminder to keep you in the present without becoming overwhelmed.

- If you are responding to something that occurs in the moment, you may want to give yourself a second to reflect on what was said or done by the other person and how you want to respond. Sometimes we falsely believe that we have to say something this second or we will never get to speak on the issue again. If the person is not a stranger walking past you on the street, you usually have a moment. Give yourself the gift of a sacred pause to gather your thoughts and check in with your feelings. Take a breath and then begin to share.

Commit to self-awareness, which is honestly and without judgment tuning into what you are feeling in the moment. Before you begin sharing, gain clarity about what you feel, and then as you share, notice if that shifts or becomes layered. For example, you may feel anger when you start a dialogue, and then as you share more, you may become aware of your sadness or fears as well. Allow yourself the freedom to feel and express the full range of your emotions.

Self-compassion is also important; meeting yourself with gentleness, understanding, and respect will give you the freedom to express yourself fully. You have been through many challenges, and your emotions are important. Communicating your feelings can be difficult, but I invite you to show up for yourself with tenderness and comfort as you feel what you feel.

Finally, consider setting parameters on your communication to ensure that you express your feelings *and* act with integrity. You may want to make some agreements with yourself in advance about what you're *not* going to do as well as what you are going to do. For example, you may commit to speaking honestly, even if it is uncomfortable, while deciding not to call the other person names, to throw things, or to make threats. This decision is not about the other person or what they did, but about your own values—how you want to live and show up in life. Your homecoming allows you to choose not to simply react to others but instead to be mindful of the ways you choose to respond.

When you express your feelings, it may also help to know and communicate what you are hoping for from the other person—empathy or comfort, for example. You may simply want to be heard, appreciated, understood, and even embraced. You may want a safe place to cry or vent without judgment. At other times, you may be looking for help with problem-solving—advice, support, or advocacy. You may want a change of behavior from that person, or you may want them to help you find a resolution. Sometimes you are actually looking for a distraction, so you call a friend to help you take your mind off an issue. Knowing what you want and expressing it can be helpful and prevent frustration. As you can imagine, if you want to be hugged but your friend is telling you to file a complaint, you may feel unsupported. Additionally, if you want distraction and the person is asking a lot of questions about what happened, you may find this upsetting as well. Communicate what you feel, and if you are aware of it, also ask for what you would like. If you're not sure what this is, that's fine, too. Friends and partners can help us with their presence even when we don't have or want a plan of action.

Emotional expression is not just about communicating with others—it's also cathartic. It may come with tears and involve journaling or even artwork. Being able to express what you feel in a poem, song, dance, prayer, or journal entry can be clarifying and empowering. When you are working hard to avoid the truth, it can drain you emotionally and even leave you physically ill—have compassion for yourself. One self-compassion posture is to place one hand on your heart and one on your belly. Another is to cross your arms over your chest, giving yourself a hug. From these positions, you can take breaths at your own pace and allow your feelings to emerge and be expressed with tears, words, or art. You can then nourish yourself in the present moment with the understanding that perfection is not the aim; rather, truth and awareness are the goal. As you are honest with yourself and others, you cultivate home in the present moment. The more we practice honest emotional expression, the less opportunity there is for stifled interactions, explosive reactions, or misunderstanding. The truth is that our silence has neither protected us from hurt feelings nor filled the empty spaces we carry. As we regularly express ourselves, we live from a place of flow instead of active suppression—and this is perpetual homecoming. For those who still feel hesitant, let me offer two points. The first is that sometimes we remain silent to keep the peace. I want to ask you whose peace you are keeping. The person who is clueless about how you feel is at peace, but you aren't. There is a difference between peace and silence. To attain authentic peace, you must be authentic. The second point is that we may fear the judgment or rejection of others when we express how we feel. If the friendship or relationship requires deception and lies, it is very fragile and may disintegrate when you both are truly honest. A fundamental part of a relationship is being known, and I hope you can cultivate spaces where you can be known fully and know others.

Let me also note that there are special considerations for self-expression if you are from a marginalized community. Whether you are marginalized because of your race, religion, gender, sexuality, or disability, some spaces are not safe for your expression. People and systems can box you in with stereotypes, stigma, and oppression. For example, Black people who express anger are more likely to be met with the fear that they will become violent. Additionally, a woman in a leadership role often faces more scrutiny about how she expresses her emotions than a man would. I would like to offer you two considerations. The first is that I hope you find or create spaces where you can express unfiltered truth without being judged. Constantly needing to perform is draining, and you will benefit from spaces where you can be yourself and be met with compassion and understanding. Second, we can often disrupt stereotypes by being our authentic selves. I once had an older Black woman mentor tell me not to smile too much with White people because they wouldn't take me seriously. She said that White people assume Black people are there to entertain them and that Black people don't provide meaningful contributions. While I fully understand the reality of those assumptions that some hold, if I live my life suppressing my joy, then I have become a prisoner to racism. I refuse to cooperate with oppression. So when I want to smile, I smile. Some will misunderstand me or dismiss me, but I cannot live freely if I am constantly calculating and contorting myself based on the false beliefs of others. I hope you also find the balance of being in safe spaces to fully express yourself and finding ways to be authentic even in the presence of those who do not value you.

## READING THE EMOTIONAL CUES OF OTHERS

While homecoming requires self-awareness, I also encourage you to consider the real value of understanding the emotional lives and experiences of others, even when they differ from your own. Assuming everyone feels what we feel is a form of disconnection. People provide social cues about their emotions, and it is important to learn to detect those cues. When we are so immersed in our own experience that we cannot imagine someone else having a different one, we are reduced to false, inauthentic interactions. If you grew up in a high-conflict home or neighborhood, it was critical for you to perceive when tension was rising so you could take the appropriate action for your safety. We all come to these skills from different places. Some of us find it easier to tune into our own feelings than to read those of others, while some are keenly aware of the emotional needs of others and less aware of their own. Wherever you find yourself with these emotional intelligence skills, know that to varying degrees you can develop them with intention and practice.

You may be more tuned into emotions in some settings than in others. If you have immersed yourself in work, you may be very skilled at picking up nuances in the workplace, but be less aware of emotional reactions in the romantic realm. If you have spent a lot of time with children, you may be very cognizant of the ways young people express their feelings but miss cues when interacting with adults. There are cultural and religious differences in emotional expression as well.

Being aware of the emotional experiences of others can aid in relationship building, vocational success, and parenting. At times, we are so caught up in our own reality that we miss what is happening with those around us. Homecoming is about being present, and when I am present with you, I take note of what is happening to you. I may enter a new job with a lot of joy and enthusiasm, but if I arrive and sense a lot of tension and burnout from others, this is important for my awareness and decision-making in that space. You may have a romantic interest in someone, but it is important to recognize if their cues reveal that they don't feel the same way. Ignoring the feelings of others can lead to confusion and disruption. While you may need to continue gathering information to understand what you are seeing or feeling in a room, you don't want to dismiss it. Those on the homecoming journey who are neurodiverse, such as those with autism or ADHD, may find these skills challenging, but as you continue to discover people who are open in communicating with you and who reject ableist or shaming responses, you may begin to notice and understand their social cues.

As we come home to ourselves, I encourage you to make a daily practice of giving consideration to how those around you are feeling. Whether they are friends, family, or coworkers, your observation and compassion can shift the interaction and perhaps even the relationship for the better.

*Denise is a fifty-four-year-old Native American woman who suffers from depression and anxiety. Because of the severity of her mental illness, she has not been able to work for over a year. One of the things she used to enjoy was event planning. Despite her challenges, she was inspired to put together an event in the hope that it would give her a renewed sense of purpose and possibility. She pressed through her distress to organize the event, which went fairly well. Despite the success, she came to a therapy session very upset with one of her friends, who was usually helpful but had disappointed her. She had asked this friend to participate in the program, but her friend said she couldn't do it. Denise felt that the friend was being selfish, inconsiderate, and ungrateful. However, based on what Denise had shared about her in previous sessions, I said, "It seems your friend may be depressed too, and she's really struggling." Denise acknowledged that the friend had previously shared her struggles with depression. I suggested the possibility that the friend's lack of participation might have had nothing to do with Denise or what she thinks of Denise, but with her feeling too overwhelmed. Denise was able to take in this feedback and acknowledge that her interpretation was more about her issues than her friend's.*

We need to be observant of our internal experience and the emotional lives of those around us. If we are not careful, we can allow our emotions to lead to incorrect assumptions about other people's intentions and thoughts. Be open and curious about the emotional lives of others, as theirs may differ from our own.

This process is complicated by the fact that people's words and actions do not always match their feelings. For example, when someone is quiet, we may assume the person is disinterested in what's going on, but they may just have social anxiety and really want to engage. Homecoming is about being present for ourselves and others in a way that gives space for the unfolding of their stories and experiences, as well as our own.

## RELATING WITH EMOTIONAL INTELLIGENCE

Learning to read emotional cues is not intended to be a tool for manipulation, but a skill that allows us to better show up with compassion and clarity. Not everyone will come right out and say they're having a rough day, so it is helpful to get a sense of the ways people manage difficult emotions. You can better navigate a conversation if you notice the other person is anxious, exhausted, or even excited. Sometimes I see clients get very frustrated because others act or feel different from them. The client will even say, "Well, if it had been me, I would have . . ." The key to remember is that the other person isn't you. Some things that come easy to you are hard for other people and vice versa. If you are an assertive, confident person, you may be puzzled by others' passivity or avoidance. It doesn't make sense to you because that is not how you work. The ability to see the world from someone else's perspective is important to being understanding of others' experiences.

This is especially true when others face stress, trauma, or disaster. We may make judgments and assumptions about how other people should cope, but we all respond to stress differently. Some become super talkative, others get very quiet; some start shopping, others start hoarding; some turn to drinking, others lose their appetite. We are unique, and I invite you to honor the unique ways in which people show the full range of their emotions. When we are not tuned into various emotional expressions, we can misread others, creating confusion and disappointment in the relationship.

We want to show up with grace and compassion for one another, recognizing that we are not clones. If everyone I interact with has to feel exactly what I feel and express it the way I would express it, I would have a very limited life experience. I'm grateful to have a diverse circle of friends who express themselves in different ways. This emotional capacity is important not just in intimate spaces but also in the wider world. Emotional intelligence empowers us not to erase ourselves or the humanity of others. From this place of awareness, we can experience home not only when we are alone but also when we are in the presence of others.

## HOMEWORK

I invite you to journal or talk with a friend about how you express your joy, anger, sadness, and anxiety. Do you feel it in your body, do you get quiet, do you get loud, or do you start to isolate and disconnect from people? See if your family or friends have noticed anything about how you express your emotions that you were not aware of. After you write or share with a friend about yourself, consider the same question for the two people closest to you. How do you know when they are having an emotional reaction to something? Does their face change? Do they tell you what they feel? Do they have a nervous laugh? Awareness of emotions and the ability to express them gets us closer to authentic living, closer to being at home with ourselves and others.

I invite your soul to tell your heart, mind, body, and spirit, "Welcome home."

# CHAPTER SIX

# Community Care and Self-Care

As we come home to ourselves, we recognize our role in the journey, as well as the impact that systems, institutions, and community have on our health and wellness. If you are being underpaid and as a result cannot afford to live in a safe neighborhood or to provide quality childcare for your children, you will need more than a bubble bath and candles for this journey. I invite us collectively to consider how we vote, advocate, organize, and care for our communities in a way that allows others to journey home to themselves, too. If we support politicians and policies that create roadblocks on the journey home for others, we are part of the problem. Instead let's be mindful of the impact our social, political, economic, and even spiritual decisions have on the well-being of cojourners trying to come home to themselves.

Caring for others, whether in the form of voting for civic-minded leaders or offering to run an errand for a neighbor, is inextricably tied to caring for yourself—we were meant to live in community, and we need each other. An important aspect of self-care is cultivating a mutually supportive community. In counseling sessions, I use a metaphor from the Old Testament and the Torah to describe the relationships we have with our communities. These ancient texts offer detailed descriptions of a temple that had an inner court and an outer court. Your closest relationship circle is like an inner court, while more peripheral relationships occupy the outer court. Some people need to remain in our outer court as general acquaintances, while others are brought into the inner court of our lives, as we grow in deeper intimacy, trust, and sharing with them. Being mindful of who you bring or keep in your inner court can be vital to your journey, as some relationships are healing and bring you closer to home, while others can drive you further away from yourself. Consider who is currently in your inner court and the level of mutual care that you provide them and they you. Set an intention for reciprocity by building and sustaining nourishing friendships, relationships that are not one-sided but ones in which you give and receive. You deserve to receive care from yourself and others. Remembering this will sustain you on the journey home to yourself.

Community psychologists, Black psychologists, and liberation psychologists talk about how the notion of self-care is very limited because it often directly or indirectly places the sole responsibility for personal wellness on an individual when we really operate as a collective. It can be a form of oppression when mental health professionals, faith leaders, and community members see you struggling but ignore all the barriers, stigma, and discrimination you face, simply concluding that you need to do better. Giving and receiving care, as opposed to the mindset that each person has to face the challenges of life alone, is a foundational aspect of community care.

We want to open ourselves to both community care and self-care rather than choosing between them. We want to cultivate healthy relationships and community support while also prioritizing our personal needs. I am *not* going to wait for other people to give me permission to nourish myself, but I will also seek out community that is nurturing. It's a beautiful thing when you can create that community. Some of you may not have those healthy connections yet, but sometimes we also need to learn how to receive support when it shows up. If you think back, there may have been moments when people were willing to help you, but you didn't want to seem weak or you didn't want them to know you needed help. Ego and pride will keep us from accepting the support of our community, so to come home to ourselves we need to lay ego aside and begin receiving.

I too have struggled to accept help. About eight years ago, I was scheduled to give a presentation at a women's professional conference in downtown Los Angeles. I was invited to speak by my dean at the university where I taught, and the opportunity was really important to me. Right when I was about to leave my house for the conference, I got a call from the sitter saying she couldn't make it. My daughter was in school, but my son was still a baby at the time. I panicked because I felt like it was too late for me to cancel. I figured that they couldn't find a new speaker in the next hour, so I decided to take my son, put him in a car seat, and drive to the hotel that was hosting the conference. As I pulled up to the venue, I looked at my son and thought, "Okay, baby boy, it's me and you." I took him out of the car seat and grabbed my laptop with my PowerPoint presentation. I was the keynote speaker, and the ballroom was full. When it was time for me to take the stage, another mother asked, "Oh, do you want me to hold your baby?" Without even considering it, I said, "No. I've got him." I stood up there and did that whole presentation holding my son. Although I was able to power through it, in retrospect, I had to think about what stopped me from canceling or receiving help.

I don't think I'm alone in this tendency to choose the superwoman model instead of allowing community to support me. Part of the journey home is learning to receive, to admit when we need support, and to be kind to ourselves. Two funny things came out of that conference. Right after it ended, another woman came up to me and said, "Oh, I wish I had known we could bring our kids. I would have brought mine." In addition, the conference photographer had taken a picture of me and my son during the presentation. We both had on orange, my favorite color, and with my permission, they ended up using the photo on the cover of their next mailing on work-life balance for women. How ironic!

Remember that when community, support, and even love show up, be open to receiving. When someone asks you what they can do to help, try not to be so quick to wave them away, declaring that you have it all under control. Whether you are dealing with a coworker, partner, or friend, allow mutuality. As you give to others, allow others to give to you. This means that we can look for ways to be a support, advocate, and giver to others, too. Let's pay attention to individuals around us who can benefit from support in addition to the systems and institutions that maintain barriers to wellness and need to be dismantled. Collectively we can shift the tide and create spaces of care and justice. Community care, or mutual care, empowers and nourishes us all for the journey home.

## SELF-CARE

Self-care involves attending to our whole selves—mind, body, and spirit. It is a radical approach to living, particularly because so many of us have, to varying degrees, been living disconnected from ourselves as a result of self-neglect or self-erasure. While many of us have experienced abandonment or neglect by others, we also need to consider whether we have neglected or abandoned ourselves physically, emotionally, or spiritually. It is often easier to recount the ways that family, friends, or romantic partners have let us down than to recognize how we have denied our own needs, feelings, or goals. If someone does not show up for us, support our dreams, understand our fears, celebrate our wins, grieve our losses, or give us time and attention, we usually recognize that they are not a good friend. But let's consider if we have been a good friend to ourselves. Have we dishonored our needs, emotions, dreams, and capacity? Have we put ourselves on the back burner while we prioritized others' needs? Have we undercut ourselves or sabotaged our success?

We can find all kinds of reasons to justify our self-neglect, as there are constant demands on our time and energy. You may have neglected your-self because you were looking out for loved ones, or because your priority was working overtime to pay the bills, or because you find it hard to give yourself permission to rest when so many are suffering, so activism takes up every inch of your life. All of these things are important *and* so are you. Your family, friends, bills, and community are worthy of care *and* so are you. If your care for others has led to your ignoring your own needs, this way of living is a hazard to your health. If everyone around you is sup-ported and you are depleted, something needs to shift so you can honor your values and obligations without betraying yourself, including your health. Self-neglect is a path to self-destruction, and if we are on that path, we are in dire need of a change of direction. Reading this book may be an alarm, a wake-up call for you. You may need to journey back to yourself. Consider the state of your body, heart, mind, and spirit.

The journey home to yourself requires placing yourself on your list of priorities. Some of you may have been raised to believe that this is selfish. As an African American and a Christian, I have often been given cultural and religious messages that say I need to always put others first. People will call you self-centered because you say no to their requests. Some will even say it is sinful or not Christlike to make your wellness a priority. While African Americans historically have been denied the space to heal, breathe, and simply be, it is important that we honor ourselves with the truth that our lives, health, wellness, and rest matter. This message applies to other marginalized groups as well. If you too are part of a faith community, I invite you to consider that observing the Sabbath, or resting while reflect-ing on the sacred, is a spiritual practice that is just as important as service. In fact, whether you consider Jesus to be a great teacher or the Messiah, he demonstrated the importance of taking time to rest and to pray. He would teach and heal, and then his disciples would wonder where he went. He would go away for restoration, so that when he was present, he could really be present. One scripture even teaches that our bodies are temples. Most faith traditions take the position that our bodies are sacred, so we need to contemplate how we have honored, cared for, and restored this temple, or conversely, how we have desecrated, neglected, or dishonored it. What an important lesson for those of us who try to perpetually pour into the lives of others, even when our pitcher is empty. Another spiritual value that we hear echoed across traditions is to love others as we love ourselves, or to treat others the way we want to be treated. We often hear that and focus on loving and treating others well but overlook the part about loving them *as* we love ourselves. Loving and caring for yourself can be a spiritual value.

For some of you, the barrier to self-care may not be related to cultural or spiritual traditions, but a history of trauma, including poverty. You may have never experienced or even witnessed someone with the luxury of stillness. Even if you have never seen it modeled, or a part of you still feels uncomfortable with paying attention to your needs, I encourage you to become more intentional about nurturing yourself emotionally, physically, and spiritually.

Audre Lorde taught us, "Caring for myself is not self-indulgence, it is self-preservation, and that is an act of political warfare." I ask you to consider who and what taught you that you were not worthy of time and care. To come home to yourself may require you to deprogram yourself from that mindset. Who is usually put in a position that requires erasing themselves? Women, people of color, LGBTQ+ community members, people with disabilities, and the impoverished, among others. It is a radical act to be still and care for yourself in a society that has bombarded you with messages of your unworthiness.

I invite you to consider:

- In what ways have you sat on your wings?
- In what ways have you minimized your voice and silenced yourself?
- When have you sought approval, validation, or attention from people who required you to be someone you're not?
- How did you abandon yourself in workspaces or relationships?

In this season, healing and coming home to yourself requires recognizing and reclaiming the parts of yourself that you left behind. Was it your courage, grief, culture, style, dreams, voice, body, spirituality, softness, playfulness, or fire? Whatever it was, go back and reclaim you.

Self-care is not only about how you speak about yourself but also how you treat yourself. You may tell me that you feel great, but as a therapist, I also want to know:

- How is your sleep?
- Do you take care of your belongings?
- Can you tolerate or even enjoy solitude?
- What has your experience with binge eating, drinking, and smoking been this week?
- What do your dating relationships look like?
- How do you feel about yourself in the presence of the person you call your best friend?
- What are you doing to cultivate your gifts?
- What are you doing to feed your mind and your spirit?

When I look at your actions, I have a better sense of how you feel about yourself. Love is a verb, an action word. We question those who tell us they love us but don't act like it. I encourage you to take a sacred pause and say to yourself, "What is the truth revealed by how I treat myself, in how I honor or dishonor myself?" If we are honest, many of us would say, "I need to work on loving myself more. I need to work on prioritizing myself." Making that declaration is not selfish. It honors the sacredness of your life. You are a precious soul that is deserving of care, rest, love, and nurturance. I know you may have received different messages from other people, but I hope a part of you can believe that truth today.

You were made in the image and likeness of the Creator of the Universe. When we really believe that, we begin to act in ways that honor our sacred identity. As you adjust how you see yourself, many other things will begin to shift as well. When you begin to accept and celebrate yourself, some decisions that you'd wrestled over become quite clear. When your wellness is a priority, some things will become intolerable, unacceptable. When you get in touch with what you feel and know, you can consult with others, but you won't need them to make all your decisions for you. As you nourish yourself, you will gain more clarity, and that is liberating. When I neglect myself, I don't know what I need, feel, or think, so I rely on other people to tell me. I want you to know there is wisdom within you. As you come home to yourself, you can more clearly hear and honor the voice within.

Approach self-care with love and tenderness. It's more than a duty or an obligation; it's an honor. So with that in mind, what have you done for you lately? In this moment, I'm not talking about whether anyone has called you or is looking out for you. Community care is important, but so is the need to nourish yourself. Some people have argued that we don't need self-care, only community care, but I disagree. Yes, we must create supportive communities, policies, and relationships, as mentioned at the beginning of the chapter, but we must also extend loving-kindness to ourselves.

If I am alive only in the presence and gaze of another, I am disconnected from myself. There will be seasons when others are not present, or when they are present but we are still absent from ourselves. On the journey home we turn away from self-neglect and disconnection from our bodies, hearts, minds, and spirits. We set an intention to be at home in our own skin and even in our soul.

Some of us have been so busy and distracted that we have lost sight of ourselves. If that's you, it can be hard to be still. It can be hard to bear silence. If I am still and silent, I may have to face some truths that I have been running from. If I am still and silent, I may have to see the parts of my life that have gone off track. Tears may come. Anger and discontent may surface if I actually stop running and sit with truth. I may even become undone. Many of us have lived buttoned-up lives, rigid and controlled, with fear just under the surface. There are some things that we would rather not know. Some things are hard to face. Your decision to pick up this book is an answer to a divine invitation, an invitation to come back home to yourself. It is a decision to say no to distraction and to say yes to yourself, yes to truth, and yes to healing. How long have you been numb, busy, distracted, disconnected? Weeks, months, years, a lifetime? However long it has been, I'm glad you're here. You honor the sacredness of your life by choosing to show up in the truth:

- You are worthy of care.
- You are deserving of self-love.
- You need nourishment not only from others but also from yourself.
- You can choose to accept yourself even when there are aspects of yourself you are still working to improve.

As you choose to love, nourish, and accept yourself, a lot of other aspects of your life will start to align or fall away. Circumstances and relationships will align with your true identity, or they may fall away, and either one is fine. Anything that cannot affirm and align with your values needs to fall away. As people come home to themselves, they may begin to tell themselves the truth about their career, the organizations they give their time to, and even their friendships. You make a decision to live truth and not a lie. You make a decision to deceive yourself no longer.

These moments of awakening and transition can be challenging but also freeing. As a professor in a graduate school program in psychology, I teach graduate students who are over thirty-five when they come to the truth that they have always wanted to be a therapist but were afraid. It is not too late for a second or even third career. They come with life experience and passion for the work. It is not too late to be who you are, either. I also work with clients who come to the realization that they have long denied the fact that certain people are not really their friends. The actions of these false friends have confirmed this fact for years, but the truth was difficult to accept. When you awaken to valuing your feelings and needs, your friendship circles shift. As you come home to yourself, be prepared for some things to fall away, shift, or arrive. Truth is a repellent and a magnet.

## PHYSICAL SELF-CARE

I invite you to think about ways you can care for yourself physically. You can think about what you eat as a self-care practice, by choosing nutritious foods and drinking plenty of water, for example. You can also think about exercise, moving your body, as a form of care. Exercise can be both preventive and corrective. If you live with diabetes, obesity, or high blood pressure, adding exercise to your life, along with addressing stress and your diet, can be very important. Even those who do not have chronic disease benefit from moving their bodies, which mental health professionals call *embodied healing* or *somatic healing* (from the Greek word *soma*, meaning the body). Instead of thinking of exercise as a dreaded chore, explore different ways of moving your body until you find one that feels enjoyable to you—whether that's walking, cycling, dancing, yoga, group sports, or even martial arts. Some parts of our healing don't come from talk therapy alone. Our bodies hold stress, memory, and even trauma, and as we move them, we begin to connect with those experiences, heal, and release.

Another aspect of physical self-care is going for regular checkups and visiting the doctor when we notice symptoms instead of waiting until it is an emergency. I know some of us face barriers around finances and insurance, but if it's feasible for you to see a doctor, going regularly is important. There have been cases of discrimination in medical practices, so if you have had a bad experience at your doctor's office, I encourage you to seek out another facility with more caring, competent, and respectful professionals.

We can also care for ourselves physically by keeping up with our hygiene, which I know can be especially challenging for those living with depression. However, any steps you can take to give yourself care and nurturance may result in lifting some of the heavy despair that you feel. This can involve the daily tasks of bathing, brushing your teeth, and changing your clothes, as well as washing and styling your hair, wearing clothes that make you feel good, doing your nails, or getting a massage. Some people think these activities are superficial, but according to behavioral psychologists, these life-affirming actions can have a ripple effect on our mind and emotions. Some people will also try to motivate you to do these things to keep your partner's interest or to attract a partner, but I would encourage you to take care of yourself for your own sake, rather than other people's. Whether you have a partner or not, whether you want a partner or not, you are deserving of care. When you take care of yourself, you may begin to feel better and to carry yourself with more confidence and a clearer sense of purpose. This is not a performance but an awakening to your worthiness and sacredness as a human being.

*Stephen was a twenty-six-year-old Latino client who came to therapy with severe grief. His father had died from cancer when Stephen was young. While he excelled academically, he suffered emotionally and socially. He was functioning in terms of his professional obligations, but he was not bathing regularly. I told him that he could continue to wait until he felt better to bathe, or he could begin bathing and see if that helped him to feel better. He could consider his visible suffering as a tribute to his father, a way of letting the world know that his father mattered and that Stephen's life would forever be changed by his father's absence, or we could explore other ways for him to honor the life of his father. When Stephen arrived for his next session the following week, he had bathed, washed his hair, and changed his clothes. There was a lift in his mood, and people had begun responding to him differently. This is not to say the grief was all gone, but Stephen was*

*closer to choosing to live, to show up to life even as he grieved his*
*father's death.*

I invite you to take any conditions off your willingness to love and nourish yourself. Some of you may be waiting until you graduate or find a partner or make a certain amount of money or lose a certain amount of weight. Can you commit to trying to love yourself in the state you're in now, with your current weight, relationship status, and finances, and with or without your family's acceptance or a particular degree?

## EMOTIONAL AND PSYCHOLOGICAL CARE

Now let's look at how you can care for your heart and mind. Emotional self-care can involve shedding toxic habits and relationships. While many sources of stress are beyond our control, we can release some of them. For example, you cannot control how family members or colleagues act, but you can often decide how much time you spend with them and how you respond to them. Sometimes we create stress for ourselves by expecting people to be different from who they really are, or we take on too much because we are not comfortable setting boundaries and telling people no. When we sign up for too much, we stretch ourselves thin and end up being resentful, exhausted, and depleted. We add to our stress when we choose to spend time with people who make us feel worse about ourselves. We know some people are not going to be kind to us based on our history with them, yet we continue to give them unlimited access to our time, energy, and self-esteem. Then we are shocked when they continue to be unkind. Can you decide today to no longer be shocked by people who are consistent in their disregard of you? It may be disappointing to recognize the truth, but as Dr. Maya Angelou has said, "When someone shows you who they are, believe them the first time." Emotional self-care involves taking your self-esteem out of the hands of those who do not care about you. If someone despises you, give yourself the gift of not waiting for their love before you can love yourself.

You can extend emotional care for yourself by making nourishing and wise decisions about where you spend your time, energy, effort, and esteem because they are valuable. You can honor and protect yourself by establishing boundaries in ways that affirm your wellness. I invite you to think about any ways you can reorder your life—including your expectations, schedule, and friendships—to decrease your stress. Consider leaving work earlier, interrupting patterns of procrastination, and recognizing the truth about the people in your family and friendship circles.

You can provide psychological care for yourself by seeking therapy and other healing pathways or practices, such as journaling, engaging in hobbies, and feeding your mind with edifying knowledge. Spending time in affirming spaces is also good for your mental health. Nourishing yourself is not a waste of time because you are not a waste of time. Consider ways you are willing to commit to nourishing your heart and mind in this season of your life.

## SOUL CARE:
## SPIRITUAL SELF-CARE

*I was meeting with Heather, a twenty-five-year-old African American graduate student. During our session, she shared the role that faith has played in her life. She had grown up in the church, although she doesn't currently belong to one. At the end of the session, I asked whether she wanted to pray together. Some clients like to integrate their faith in their sessions, and some do not. She indicated that she would like that, so we prayed together, and at the end, as I lifted my head and opened my eyes, I saw that she was crying and rocking back and forth. She said, "Thank you so much. I haven't had anyone pray with me since my grandmother died. I didn't know how much I missed that."*

On a deep level, there is an essence to who you are that is much more than the sum total of your experiences. You have a spirit and a soul. You can spend time spiritually edifying and nourishing yourself so you can go beyond the motions of living and truly come alive. I have a spoken word piece that goes, "Why walk when you can fly? *Why walk when you can fly?* What are you doing on your knees, dragging wings?" Your soul has the capacity to take flight. You have spiritual gifts, and the reality is that you're too gifted to be bored. Spiritual gifts include but are not limited to wisdom and discernment, faith, healing, teaching, giving, leading, and serving. If you're bored, it means that some of your spiritual gifts have been asleep. There are rich layers within each of us, and when you become aware of all that is within you, hidden treasures rise to the surface. The stress and trauma of life may have kept you from seeing the bounty within you and may even have convinced you that you are an empty shell. There is a part of you that you may be neglecting; you may have never been introduced to your spirit or you may have lost sight of it, but it is important. Your spirit is a part of you, and in this homecoming, we don't want to leave any part of ourselves behind. A part of your homecoming is awakening your spirit, or as we say in my faith tradition, "Stir up the gifts." Your spiritual gifts may have been dormant for a long time, but there is more to you than your body, your mental health, and even your heart. We can think of soul care as activating your spirit; awakening and raising your consciousness is the path to holistic wellness.

How do you awaken spiritually? How do you connect with your spiritual gifts? You start by spending time in meditation or prayer. You may also read sacred texts, engage with the arts, pursue your purpose, align your life with your values, and utilize your spiritual gifts. We do not all have *every* gift, but we all have *a* gift. You can start utilizing your gifts as a way to nourish yourself so you are no longer holding back but living life in flow and alignment with who you are and what gifts you carry. Additionally, a part of soul care is using wisdom in selecting spiritual communities who nourish your soul. If the aim of your spiritual tradition is love and connection, but your community leaves you feeling rejected and disconnected, this may not be a place of growth and healing for you. All communities are made up of flawed people, so the aim is not perfection but a community in which there is honesty, accountability, safety, affirmation, and growth. A part of your soul care may involve leaving or transforming a community, or finding new places where your soul is fed and where you can also be a part of helping others. If you have been hurt in a spiritual or religious community, soul care may mean stepping away from community for a season as you heal and eventually deciding if you are open to exploring different, safer spaces. It's important to know that one tradition doesn't have a monopoly on harm or abusive practices. People have been hurt in temples, churches, mosques, spiritual centers, meditation groups, and yoga classes. So if you are seeking community, look at the words and actions of the leaders, teachers, and members, and pay attention to how your spirit feels when you are present and when you leave. The aim of soul care is to be nourished, edified, renewed, enlightened, and loved.

## BARRIERS TO SELF-CARE

There are countless ways you can engage in self-care—whether it's walking in nature, blowing bubbles, playing with kids, creating beautiful art, cooking a healthy meal, or spending time with friends and family. As books on time management will tell you, people make time for what matters to them. As a psychologist and minister, I would love for you to consider how much you matter to yourself. Do you believe that you're worthy of care? For some of you, the deeper issue is not that you don't know how to exercise self-care or don't have time, but that somewhere along the way you came to believe you were not deserving of care. You may have been given the message that your needs aren't important or that you would be a better person if you didn't have any needs. Take a moment to consider the experiences and people that made you feel that way. Think about who you believe to be deserving of care and how you go about addressing their needs—whether it's your partner, children, or friends. Then consider how your life would look different if you really loved, cherished, honored, accepted, and valued yourself. You don't have to like everything about yourself to care for yourself. We are all works in process, but the requirement for care should not be perfection.

For the journey home, push past the feelings of unworthiness so you can begin regularly feeding your spirit, protecting your mental health, and nourishing your body. I invite you to make your wellness a priority and no longer give all of your time and energy away. I invite you to reprogram the mindset that taught you that protecting time for yourself was wrong. As you develop a healthy appetite for your growth and wellness, it will become easier to say no to requests that do not align with your values. The more you say no to those things, the more space you will have in your life for the things that feed, grow, and liberate you to be fully who you are. Some of those yeses are not just for new obligations; save a yes for a nap, a walk, a long bath, or a funny show. Set aside a yes for journaling, meditating, nourishing your relationships, and listening to music.

## HOMEWORK

A few years ago, I was the psychologist on the Oprah Winfrey Network TV show *Chad Loves Michelle* with sports chaplain Chad Johnson and Destiny's Child singer Michelle Williams. In one of their couples sessions, I gave them a homework assignment to write vows to themselves. I would like to offer that homework to you for this chapter. Many of us are waiting for others to make or honor promises to us. As you consider your journey home, you must make some commitments to yourself. Traditionally when people get married, they vow to love each other in sickness and in health, for richer or for poorer, for better or for worse. They vow to honor and cherish each other above anyone else for the rest of their lives. What are some promises you want to make to yourself going forward and for the rest of your life? You may want to commit to loving yourself in success and in failure, whatever the size and shape of your body, whether you are in a relationship or single, when those around you celebrate you and when they reject you. You may want to commit to not erasing or abandoning yourself in pursuit of someone else's attention or approval. Perhaps you can make a vow to show yourself compassion whether you're laid off or promoted, when you're on top of things and when procrastination or depression have you depleted. Vow to love yourself, including your race, gender, sexuality, disability, income, and age. Vow to love your mind, heart, body, and spirit. You may want to make a sacred vow to give yourself rest and permission to be imperfect, tired, overwhelmed, disappointed, and frustrated, as well as joyful, excited, and loved. Finally you may want to vow to forgive yourself and reclaim your voice and your life. Before going on to the next chapter, I invite you to write your vows, and if you have a trusted friend, you may want to share your vows with them. If not, reading your vows to yourself can be a sacred, healing ritual.

After all you have survived, may today be the day your soul tells your heart, mind, body, and spirit, "Welcome home."

# CHAPTER SEVEN

# Building Self-Confidence

*Throughout graduate school, I attended psychology conferences to learn and network with those in the field. Every year I would look through the conference program for panels related to mental health in Africa. I was interested in international psychology as a result of both my heritage as an African American and the years I spent living in West Africa as an adolescent. There would usually be one or two programs focused on Africa, often chaired by Dr. Corann Okorodudu, a Liberian American psychologist. The programs were often scheduled at eight a.m., and only a handful of people would attend. Soon after I graduated with my doctorate, I saw an advertisement in the American Psychological Association (APA)* Monitor *magazine for psychologists to serve as mental health representatives at the United Nations. I was a recent graduate, so I thought my chances were slim, but I decided to apply anyway. I thought that if they didn't pick me as a primary representative, they might still let me shadow someone as a trainee. I reasoned that the worst that could happen was that they would turn me down. I believed that my passionate commitment to the study of Africa and the Diaspora and my experience in*

*Liberia could contribute to the work. I applied and was selected among only a handful of representatives. It turns out the UN was about to have a world conference on the elimination of racism, and I was the only applicant who mentioned the psychology of racism in my statement of interest. That was about twenty years ago, and I am so glad I had the confidence to apply. This opportunity opened many doors for me to engage in international advocacy, research, and intervention. In 2020, I was honored with an award for international contributions to the psychology of women and gender by the American Psychological Association. If I'd surrendered to the fear that I was not enough, I would have missed my entrance into this purposeful work.*

As you journey home to yourself, feelings of insecurity and intimidation can slow you down and cause you to spend years living beneath your potential. To reach your full capacity, you have to stretch outside of your fears, anxieties, and self-doubt. When you lack confidence, it diminishes your view of yourself by creating and sustaining shame-based mindsets and decision-making.

On the other hand, confidence can open doors for you and empower you to move in the direction of your dreams. When you lack confidence, you often focus on your limitations or contrast what you can do with what other people can do, but you can accomplish some incredible things just as you are right at this moment. More important, confidence allows you to simply be at peace with who you are right now. I invite you to take a sacred pause and think about what you have already overcome and what you have survived. All the things you have lived through can sometimes cast a shadow over your view of yourself, blocking you from seeing what it took for you to get where you are. Remembering what you have already survived can inspire you to have the confidence to face whatever mountain, ocean, or challenge is in front of you.

## BUILDING CONFIDENCE ON PAST EXPERIENCES

When we get intimidated in the present, we are often operating out of amnesia. We have forgotten who we are and what we have already gone through. Whatever your age, you have experiences that serve as the foundation for confidence. I invite you to tap into the survivor spirit in you. Tap into your resilience by recalling your track record for recovering after a crash. I invite you to tap into the wisdom you carry, which is demonstrated by your history of walking through some terrifying circumstances and coming out on the other side. If you remember who you are and what you have come through with clarity, it will give you some courage and confidence.

The confidence you grow in your homecoming journey does not appear out of thin air. Sometimes when people ask how they can become more confident, they are expecting something magical. This is not magic. Your confidence should be rooted in the truth of your life. Confidence is not built on a fantasy. The homecoming invitation is an offer for you to believe in the self that has already survived all the events, seasons, and years of your life. I invite you to have confidence in your spirit, heart, and mind based on your track record. Your track record doesn't have to be perfect— in fact some failures prepare us for later successes if we pull the wisdom out of the experiences. Even if you have not experienced a challenge directly, you may have a related experience you can build on, or you may have observed someone in that position, which gives you insight.

Whatever you've experienced has given you some building blocks. The blocks may be rough, cracked, and overlooked, but your hands are not empty. You are not empty. You have passion, knowledge, life experience, and the capacity to survive. You have grown from your history, and that history—the wins and losses—can give you some confidence to face your present circumstance.

Some situations may have caused you to doubt and judge yourself, but to build confidence, you need to acknowledge your missteps and then develop some insight about what led you to a dead end. The way you grow your confidence is by recognizing and understanding with clarity and compassion who you were before. Based on your wisdom and knowledge about the past, you can make some different decisions in the future. You can grow and shift in your present, instead of judging yourself harshly and remaining stuck in your past. Remember that failure is an event, not an identity. If you have failed in the past, you can learn from it and carry that wisdom and knowledge into your future. Reject the idea that past failures make you a failure. When you think of failure as your identity, it keeps you stuck. When you see failure as an event, you can grieve, dissect it, and learn from it without being defined by it.

I am not encouraging you to ignore your past but to learn from it. For example, if you do not have confidence in your ability to have healthy relationships because of past negative experiences, then you may benefit from asking yourself what was going on within you and around you that contributed to your being in unhealthy relationships. With grace and without judgment, consider what you now know about yourself and your relationships that you did not know back then. Your new insight can serve as the foundation for growing your confidence. In this way, the confidence doesn't have to be based on what you have already attained but on what you now perceive that you didn't before. You can move from judgment to wisdom by pulling the lessons out of those wounds, regrets, failures, and pits.

Instead of defining yourself by the times when you fell short, you can recognize the ways in which you have grown since then. As you look back on those past seasons, reflect on:

- What you were feeling
- What you were thinking
- Why you made the choice(s) you made
- What prior experiences shaped how you responded

- What insecurities or self-doubts influenced your thinking
- How you saw yourself during that time
- Who or what made you feel something was acceptable that you now believe is unacceptable
- What you got right or appreciate about your former self
- What, if anything, in that situation was a win, breakthrough, or awakening

Your confidence today can be based in part on the insight that arose from evaluating your past successes and failures, gains and losses. When you start operating out of your hard-earned wisdom, you can prevent yourself from walking into traps like those you have already fallen into. Think back on some circumstances, perhaps at work or with family, where a situation was a mess *and* you participated in the mess-making. But if that same bait, same mess, was to show up again, you would see it for what it was and not get caught up in it.

Can you be honest in this moment and acknowledge that you did some things, picked up habits, and went down paths that were not helpful? You may have been in dating relationships that were not enriching. So your confidence is not based on having lived a perfect life, but a life full of growth. You can have confidence based on your wins as well as on living a full life that includes the opportunity to learn from your mistakes.

*Early in my career, I had the opportunity to go on a panel-format television program. Right before we went on the air, the producer came out to give the panel a pep talk. He said that they liked the show to be high-energy and didn't want any dead air, so if someone made a point and we had a related thought, he invited us to just jump in there and keep our energy high. Being the people pleaser that I was at that point in my life, I took those instructions to heart. I jumped in on people's comments. I made all my points with maximum emotion and energy. I did as I was told.*

*Well done, right? Wrong. When I watched the program, I didn't like the Thema who showed up that day. No one watching the show heard those instructions from the producer. They just saw the panelists. We looked rude, over the top, and ridiculous. I was disappointed in myself for taking the bait and behaving in a way that was not consistent with my values or personality.*

The great thing about life is that sometimes you get a do-over, which I like to call a divine retest. A few years later, I was invited on another panel where all the guests were lawyers and I was the only psychologist. The producer of that program pulled me aside before the taping and basically gave me the same pep talk. This time I didn't listen. I spoke and showed up in a way that was consistent with who I am and how I show up in other spaces of my life. I was not concerned about the producer's opinion of me. I was committed to honoring the truth of who I am. I wasn't the most dramatic guest, but I was invited to come back several more times. Even if I had never been invited back again, being myself was the win. I had the confidence to learn from the past and choose my inner wisdom in the present.

While past success can build your confidence, there is also something to be gained from our missteps. This is perhaps why many people in drug and alcohol recovery prefer to have a sponsor—someone who mentors a person newer to the recovery process. Similarly, some people who have had relationships that didn't work out can share wisdom gained from those experiences. Some people who have struggled with health conditions or financial difficulties can provide insight that those who have had perfect health and a perfect credit score may not have.

Building confidence from the past requires that we see and speak truth. A few years ago, I ran into a woman I know with her teenage daughter. They had recently moved out of a domestic violence shelter and were renting a room in a house. The woman shared excitedly that she had a new man in her life. She was beaming, but her daughter, who was standing behind her, was smirking, rolling her eyes, and shaking her head. The woman was enthusiastically telling me that she knew the man from high school and had reconnected with him online. She said that he would be back home next year, so I asked if he was away in the military. She said no, he was incarcerated. She was quick to tell me how spiritual he was and how she was sure I would like him. Her daughter stood behind her, glaring at her and looking at me as if to say, "Can you believe this?" I asked about the charge he was serving time for, and she said it was for attempted murder of his girlfriend, but quickly explained that he pulled the weapon out only because he caught the girlfriend cheating on him. As I began to talk to the mother about how she deserves peace and safety, I was reminded of another reality. While the mother still could not see the pit she was in, her daughter, who was less than sixteen, could see it clearly. The truth is that some of the confidence and wisdom that we have comes not just from what we have lived through directly but also from what we have witnessed. This baby girl had already witnessed the violence that landed them in a shelter, and now she had the confidence and clarity to know when she was looking at a pit, even when her mother was in denial. As you look back on your life, perhaps some confidence came not only from what you survived directly but also from what you saw. May you be empowered by those experiences, instead of believing that they create limits as to what's possible for you. You can grow beyond your past, and even grow from the lives of those who raised you.

## SELF-COMPASSION FOR NEW BEGINNINGS

I tell my graduate students who are studying to become psychologists that when they first start seeing clients, most training sites are very protective of them and the clients. They are often assigned clients who are considered "high functioning" and who may have challenges related to everyday sources of stress or relationship problems but are not in a current crisis. This was the way my training started. I had clients who had past trauma or current stress, but overall, they were considered a good match for a clinician in training. When I left my graduate school training site and moved to Boston for my internship, I was startled when I was assigned my first client living with schizophrenia, my first client who was actively suicidal, and my first client who was living with dissociative identity disorder. I was understandably insecure because these were new challenges. I was afraid I would say or do the wrong thing. I was intimidated and lacked confidence. Approaching this work with humility was important, as people's lives and mental health are important and need to be honored and cared for appropriately. Now that I have spent two decades in the field, when people come to me with diverse issues and conditions, I am not intimidated anymore, but I remain humbled by people's willingness to allow me to journey with them in their healing and growth. Because I have more experience, I can understand what I see when I'm working with clients, and as a result, I have more confidence about what we can accomplish together.

I share this story because sometimes you may feel bad about lacking confidence, but I want to invite you to give yourself grace about what you don't know. Whether you are new to a career or to parenting or to romance, give yourself compassion as you grow and learn. If you are comparing yourself to people who have more experience, you're setting yourself up for frustration and insecurity. Instead, be patient with yourself and set realistic expectations for where you are in your journey. When you have never done something before or have not been doing it long, you need to allow for growing pains—the discomfort of adjustment and the awkwardness that comes with newness.

An experience is also new if you are trying to approach it in a healthier way than before. For example, if you are trying love without defensiveness and intimacy without intoxication for the first time, or even launching a business after years of working for other people, give yourself growing room. Initially you're likely going to feel anxiety and self-doubt, but don't retreat simply because you're nervous. Allow yourself to move forward, because sometimes you have to proceed in spite of being scared. You gain confidence and experience by acting even when you're intimidated. Can you commit today to outlasting your self-doubt? With time and experience, your knowledge and wisdom will grow. New beginnings are usually full of the unfamiliar and the uncomfortable, but that is *not* a sign that you are incapable.

Being in a new environment, whether physically or psychologically, is difficult for many of us. The unfamiliar may bring up fears of being out of control. It may be easier to be the expert, but being a beginner can be refreshing and exciting. If you can release the need to be in control, to appear to know everything, or to be the leader, you can experience the joy of learning and growing in confidence over time.

Building your confidence requires a willingness to be in some spaces where you're not the expert, but where you are teachable. You might think confidence is about authority and having all the answers, but growing your confidence requires you to tolerate being a newcomer. Just keep pressing on through the insecurity and keep learning. As you continue to gain experience, the confidence will grow. Many times, we want instant confidence, something that emerges overnight with one mantra, one workbook exercise, one pronouncement from a guru. Some spiritual spaces will tell you to turn around three times, and some intellectuals will tell you to read a specific book. But I offer you the truth. Authentic confidence is not instant. It can grow over time. The more you engage in life, particularly in the area of your insecurity, the more your confidence is built up. It is also important to be conscious of the time that has been committed to tearing down your confidence. If you had a childhood, adolescence, and adulthood when people and events were constantly chipping away at your confidence or even preventing it from developing, it will undoubtedly take a commitment over time to restore it.

## EARLY EXPOSURE

For those who are parents, it's a beautiful thing to expose your children to affirming experiences early on, so they develop confidence from the beginning, before they can be told that they should be afraid of things. It is easier to teach babies and young children to learn a new language or swim. When you approach newness with curiosity and openness instead of insecurity, you have more confidence to step into the unknown. Although you are not a child anymore, if you allow yourself to learn and grow, you will increase your confidence to try new things. Growth is a process and a journey, so you need the confidence to take one step at a time, trusting that the path and the destination are real possibilities.

Your family of origin can give you an inheritance of confidence or one of self-doubt. However, even if they gave you the weight of insecurity, that does not mean you have to continue to carry it. You can break generational cycles and choose not to pass these anxieties down to your children.

A good friend of mine had an intense fear of dogs. She had always accepted that fear as a part of her identity. As a child, she saw a dog attack one of her neighbors. From that point onward, she felt intense dread and fear whenever she was in the presence of a dog, so she did her best to avoid them. However, once she became a mom and saw how severe her son's fear of dogs was, she felt horrible. She did not want her son to be controlled by this trepidation in the way that she had been. She actively began working to overcome her anxieties regarding dogs. As she overcame her unease, her son, following her example, overcame his unease as well.

I hope you will be mindful of the insecurities, fears, and doubts handed down to you directly or indirectly. Then you can begin to distinguish between what was given to you and who you actually are, and differentiate between your anxiety and your identity.

# ONE STEP AT A TIME

*Joshua is a visionary. Every few years he is inspired to take on a huge initiative. The vision often exceeds his budget and requires a lot of labor from people whom he cannot afford to pay. At the end of the project, he is usually frustrated. People who were working with him are burned out and disappear; and the end result, while commendable to outsiders, always falls short of Joshua's vision. Initially Joshua was inflexible in terms of his willingness to adjust the visions he had. He saw dreaming smaller as a failure and a form of surrender. As we began to look at the practical reality of how and why his visions often fell short, he began to be more open to exploring other approaches. We also had to look at his early life experiences that had given him such a need to prove himself to the world and even to himself. Over time, with patience and insight, Joshua was able to envision an endeavor that matched his budget, time, and resources. When he met this goal, I encouraged him to resist the tendency to focus on all the ways it could have gone better and to actually learn to enjoy the win. With self-reflection, he was able to see and appreciate the success, experience an authentic boost in his confidence, and then look at ways to build on the vision for the next iteration.*

There are times when you may have sabotaged your confidence by setting the first bar too high. When you are facing a fear, psychologists recommend gradual exposure. You might start off by just visualizing in your mind what you are afraid of. Then you might look at pictures or videos of the source of your fear. Later, you might just be in the room with what you fear without actually approaching it. Eventually you work up the confidence to pet the animal, ride the elevator, take the flight, or make the speech in front of an audience.

You may feel insecure because your initial attempt was too big a step. If you have a fear of water, you may want to just sit and look at the pool or put your feet in before you try to dive into the deep end and swim. Similarly, in relationships, if your tendency is to declare that someone you meet is your soul mate without first developing a friendship, you may find yourself repeatedly devastated if the relationship doesn't last. In school, some people try one semester in which they register for challenging courses they were not prepared for and then decide they are not "college material." Before you write yourself off or dismiss your dreams, you may want to create some smaller goals that will eventually position you to succeed at the larger goal.

When I became a university professor, I had to learn about the publishing process for academic journals. The article you submit is reviewed by scholars in your area of expertise. Very rarely do the reviewers give a first submission an immediate acceptance. The usual review decision for a first submission is a "revise and resubmit." You are given a list of suggestions of ways you can or need to improve the article. When you first start, opening one of these letters can be discouraging and overwhelming. The more experience you have, the more you realize that most of the suggestions you receive are intended to help your article become stronger, which benefits you. You review the feedback, making corrections or explanations one item at a time, and usually your article is eventually accepted for publication. If, however, you open that letter of evaluation and conclude that you are not a good writer, so there is no need to bother with the corrections, you will never be published. Then we have a self-fulfilling prophecy. You decided you don't have what it takes, so you stop trying. Then your career reflects the assumption you made about yourself.

When you keep showing up to life despite the insecurity and fear of embarrassment or failure, you eventually build your confidence. Some of the things you used to be intimidated by you don't even consider difficult anymore. Keep taking baby steps in the direction of the life you want and the way in which you want to show up for yourself. Do not set the bar so high that you guarantee falling short. Instead, train yourself to recognize small steps of progress along the way. When you can see the wins that you may have overlooked in the past, your confidence will grow.

A therapist or insightful friend can also help you see your successes. In therapy, I empower clients to take another look at their life journey—this time, with compassion. Some of the ways you survived may be rough, awkward, or even embarrassing, but you made it, and I'm glad you're still here. Even if you want to change and grow, you can still give yourself patience, grace, and appreciation for the ways in which you made it this far.

## ENCOURAGERS AND DISCOURAGERS

*Priya is a creative person who also works in the corporate world. A few years ago, she was working on a huge creative project. Since she spends time every weekend with her mother, I was surprised to discover she had not told her mom about the project. Priya shared with me that her mother's anxiety makes her unsupportive of any risky initiatives. Priya said, "To finish the project, I couldn't tell my mom. She would shoot holes in the idea and make me doubt myself, so it would never get done." Priya disclosed that her mother is the type of person you can tell good news to only once it is already finished and other people are celebrating it. So when the project was complete and there was a big celebration, Priya invited her mother. Priya discovered this formula for reaching her dreams only after many childhood and adult years during which her mother discouraged her and talked her out of her potential. This experience resulted in painful seasons and a strained relationship. But through therapy, supportive friends, limits on what she shares with her mother, and a habit of bearing witness to her own success, Priya has been able to build her confidence.*

Be mindful of the messages you tell yourself, as well what those around you say, because they can discourage or encourage you. You may feel insecure because of the discouragers in your life. Whether they are relatives, teachers, guidance counselors, former supervisors, or colleagues, discouragers intentionally break your confidence. While this is very painful, it is also liberating to realize you can change your circle to spend more time in the company of encouragers. The people you surround yourself with can help build your confidence. When possible, spend less time with people who heighten your insecurity and more time with those who inspire, motivate, enhance, and affirm your abilities. It is hard to heal your self-confidence if you continue to spend time with people who undermine and discourage you.

You may need to take inventory of those around you to consider how you feel while you are in their presence and when you leave their presence. Often, as you begin to build your confidence, there will be a ripple effect, and those around you will become more courageous and confident as well. Boldness can be contagious. You do not have to live your life shading your shine by playing it safe and underutilizing your gifts, no matter how many years you have been living beneath your potential. Homecoming gives you permission to embrace the confidence to step into the radiance of truth beyond self-doubt. As you come home to yourself, you will recognize more clearly and quickly connections that support the development of your confidence and those that undermine it. Make decisions about how you invest your time and energy with this in mind.

There are people you share your dreams with who will encourage the journey even if they acknowledge that it may not be easy. There are others whose words and attitudes can leave you feeling deflated, more insecure, and more self-doubting. Of course, authentic friends can and should give genuine feedback, but overall you want to assess the impact of a friendship or relationship on your sense of self-worth. If your aim is to build or rebuild your confidence, become intentional about cultivating a life with actions and relationships that support that aspiration. Get in the presence of those who will celebrate your wins and who can remind you that your failures are not the end of your story.

## HOMEWORK

------------------------------------------------------------------

Journal or share with a friend or therapist the progress you have made over the last five years. Those years may include some stumbles or even total collapse, but there has also been some growth. There is some awareness now that was not present before. You were faced with some difficult moments that you handled with more clarity, calm, insight, or compassion than you would have five years ago. You may also have some skills now that you didn't have before. What did you learn through your job, reading, relationships, therapy, or spiritual practices? What are the things that you weren't sure you would survive over these years, and yet here you are? What are the things that dismantled you but did not end you? As you journal or share, be sure to take in the growth with compassion, knowing that your confidence can authentically grow the more you look over your life with understanding instead of judgment. The beautiful part about building confidence is realizing you don't need to be a pillar of perfection overnight. Instead you can be a human being with flaws and mistakes who continues to grow in confidence day by day.

The truth about the psychological and spiritual muscles and skills you're developing now is that you already have evidence to support your growing confidence. Celebrate yourself along the way instead of waiting to become some drastically different person in order to know that you are worthy.

If it feels right for you:

Breathe in confidence from the lessons you've learned.

Breathe out insecurity from the wounds you've experienced.

I invite your soul to tell your heart, mind, body, and spirit, "Welcome home."

# CHAPTER EIGHT

# Spiritual Practices

*Growing up, I was blessed to watch a phenomenal woman up close: my mother. Her name is Reverend Cecelia Williams Bryant, and she is a mystic, a poet, an author, a minister, and an intercessor who commits her time to praying for and ministering to others. Starting in the 1970s, my mother began hosting conferences for women of African descent to connect with the sacredness of their identity. There is so much anti-Black racism and so much ridicule of Black women in particular. My mom has spent her life working to nourish the spirits of African and Diasporic women. She was instrumental in creating an outreach center, an associate degree program, a women's center, and numerous women's spiritual retreats. Over forty years, she hosted conferences in the United States and other countries. These gatherings incorporated the arts; practical services to address the housing, medical, employment, and educational needs of women and girls in the area; opportunities to learn how to have healthy, affirming relationships with other women; and spiritual disciplines. I witnessed the emotional and spiritual awakening, healing, and empowerment of Black women from all walks of life who came in burdened and left renewed with a sense of hope, connection, and, most important, awareness that they were sacred and beloved.*

*My mother was raised by my grandfather, a World War II veteran named Booker T. Williams, and my grandmother, a phenomenal woman named Mrs. Pauline Lucas Williams. My grandmother had the same gift of empowering people to know how special they are. She worked for many years at an orphanage in New York, where she lovingly cared for children who had been discarded, neglected, and abused, and let them know they were seen, appreciated, and worthy. I may be the first PhD psychologist in my family, but I am not the first member of my family to facilitate healing. One of the gifts of doing this work is that it blesses us as we seek to be a blessing to others. I was raised to know healing work is not just what you learn in a book or do for a paycheck. Healing is a spiritual matter, and that happens in the heart and spirit, not just the head.*

To journey home to yourself requires a decolonizing of psychology, which means paying attention to our cultural context, both historically and in the present moment. Decolonizing psychology also involves indigenizing psychology, recognizing the ways people have grown and healed before the field of psychology even existed and the diverse ways people continue to grow and heal. One of those pathways to growth and healing is developing your spirituality. To come home to yourself with the wisdom of those who came before you involves acknowledging that you are a spiritual being.

Several common principles across faith traditions will help us on the journey home. Let us begin by taking a moment of silent reflection, centering in on our breath. For some of you, that breath connects you to your Creator; for others, it may connect you to yourself or to gratitude for life.

As you become aware of your breath at your own pace, tune into your appreciation for this moment, the gift of presence. There are those who came before us who did not have the luxury of stillness, healing, and sustained, intentional self-care. This moment is a gift that has been provided in part by their sacrifices, as well as a gift you have chosen to utilize.

There are many running around trying to win in life by competition and incessant accumulation of possessions and superficial friendships, repeating stale cycles that end with emptiness. I honor your inner spirit that has come to this journey as a result of choosing to show up for your inner life, of becoming aware of the sacredness of your life. So together we can center in on some key principles that will help you return home to recover and heal.

## SIMPLICITY AND LIVING IN THE PRESENT

As a woman of African descent, I know sometimes culturally we like to be extra and we celebrate being extra—vibrantly expressive in our fashion, music, speech, and even hairstyles. I love it. My favorite color is orange, and I love the sound of drums and soul singers. I love listening to gifted storytellers who weave past with present with hypnotic enthusiasm in pulpits, on hip-hop stages, in corporate spaces, and on street corners. I love performing spoken word and African dance. I love the juiciness of being a Black woman. *And* there is also a gift in discovering that none of the extra captures the fullness of me. There are aspects of me, aspects of all of us that are unspoken and unseen. In these simple moments, I come to acknowledge and appreciate parts of myself that others may not readily see. In the simplicity of stillness and silence, I come home to the truth of who I am. When I turn down the volume and lay down at night, when I see Black women kneeling at altars, when I see Black girls daydreaming, I am reminded of the richness of our interior lives. The beauty and power there is often unrecognized by others and sometimes even by us.

This is true for you, too. There is a deep well within you, within each of us, that sometimes we miss with the busyness of life. After everything you have experienced, gained, and lost over the course of your life, you are finally ready to do the necessary work of clarifying who you are on the inside. You lost some of the things or people you thought you could not live without, yet here you are, still breathing, still here.

You have awakened to the reality or have always known that materialism is not going to fill you up. A bunch of name brands is not going to satisfy your soul. Impressing other people is not as satisfying as some might think. You come to the place of realizing your inherent worth, which isn't tied to possessions or accomplishments—as the incredible Black playwright and poet Ntozake Shange discovered after dealing with depression, alienation, and the feeling of living a lie. She decided to adopt the Zulu name Ntozake, which means "she who comes with her own things." It is so important that you come to a place where you can see and celebrate the part of you no one can take away. The essence of who you are is yours. You may have lost sight of it, and it may have been neglected, but under all the challenges of life, you are still there. This is not borrowed, manufactured, imitated, or duplicated. This part of you does not need the justification or approval of the crowd. I see you coming to this journey, and your hands and heart are not empty. Your mind is not empty, and your spirit is definitely not empty. You come possessing your own things, and those things are more than the bruises and scars of your yesterday. It is your core, your spirit; and I celebrate who you are on the inside. Even with the difficulties, the frailties, and the imperfections, you are a living soul.

Some things may have been removed from your life, misplaced, stolen, or given away, but remember that you are quite simply enough. Your presence, your voice, and your gifts are enough. This moment is enough. Decide to live in the simplicity of now, to live in the present. Many times we are caught up in regret about the past or anxiety about the future, but I invite you to participate in the spiritual practice of recognizing the sacredness of now. This moment, the now, is more than what has been done in your past, and it has the power to shape your future. Embrace the sacredness of this moment.

Often we are so busy trying to get somewhere, trying to become someone, that we miss the beauty of right now. While it is valuable to have goals and dreams, I wonder if you're able to accept yourself in your present condition. I wonder if you can celebrate yourself in your present condition, beyond the striving of what and who you shall be, but who you are right now.

With the beauty of simplicity in the present moment, you can start to reconnect with who you are on the inside.

## INTERCONNECTION

Another spiritual principle is being aware that we are connected with all living beings. This consciousness of our interconnectedness can break down any sense of isolation. It counters the lies and the myths that no one will ever understand, appreciate, or care about you. Interconnection shifts the idea that your life doesn't matter. Each person, each living being is a reflection, a component, a branch in the larger tree of life. When you can shift your understanding of your connection to others, the load you carry can lighten. You no longer need to feel that you alone carry the weight of the world on your shoulders. You may have been journeying through life believing that all the weight of responsibility has landed on you and that there is no one you can confide in, that no one will understand. But the truth is, you are not in that experience alone. The dynamics and details vary from person to person, but there are others with similar thoughts and feelings.

I invite you to consider our collective experience, connection, relationships, and humanity. As you come home to yourself, you get a more realistic sense of awareness beyond you. You can reject the narrow idea that it's you against the world or that you have to figure everything out by yourself. We are all on the journey—some walking, some crawling, some dragging their feet, and some running—but our presence has an impact, a significance. We are all in this process of unfolding and becoming.

Be gracious when you see someone else on the journey, knowing that even though you don't have access to their whole story, we all have a story. You can give grace to yourself and to others, give permission for the imperfections along the way. You don't have to be a superhero. You can cease comparing your wounds to the assumed perfection and ease of others. We are all sacred beings and have human experiences.

*Shannon is a single Black woman who works in a corporation with very few people of color. She isolates herself at work to avoid the insensitive, discriminatory comments of colleagues. Her family is emotionally draining, so she intentionally spends very little time with them. Her friends care about her, but she doesn't really let them know her on a deep level. She has mastered having conversations without disclosing very much about herself. She spends a lot of time alone and feels quite misunderstood and isolated. Her spirituality is important to her, but it has largely been a solitary journey for her as an adult. A major roadblock on her homecoming journey was unprocessed grief. As she gave herself permission to grieve in therapy, she began to see and appreciate her desire to connect with others more authentically. Her relationships with select coworkers deepened, as well as her communication with and connection to family and friends. She eventually also acknowledged a desire for companionship, which previously she was not willing to consider. As Shannon shared both her faith and her sorrow more honestly, she gained strength to continue to journey back home to her authentic self.*

## MINDFULNESS AND CONTEMPLATIVE PRACTICE

Related to simplicity and connectivity is the notion of mindfulness, which is inspired by teachings from Asian cultures and religion, specifically Buddhism. Mindfulness meditation as a wellness philosophy, practice, and approach to living is now popular in the United States, and was developed within the field of psychology by Jon Kabat-Zinn. Mindfulness can be defined as intentionally tapping into your awareness in the present moment with compassion. It is more than just meditating for a few minutes a day. It is a way of living with awareness, generosity, and connection. Currently there are Buddhist, Christian, and secular forms of mindfulness, to name a few. Predating American notions of mindfulness was contemplative practice, including Christian contemplative traditions of recognizing stillness and silence as vital to an ongoing connection to the presence of God. There is also Soulfulness, an approach rooted in African American cultural aliveness, spirituality, and connection developed by psychologist Dr. Shelly Harrell.

Some have noted the commodification, commercialization, whitewashing, and divorcing of mindfulness from its spiritual and cultural roots. This trend is popular in the Western world, where many will try to disconnect a practice from its spiritual or religious roots and use it as a tool to be more productive, to increase one's focus, or to improve one's health. The gift of spiritual awareness in the present moment is much more valuable than a path to gain more things (money, years, reputation, etc.). It is a way of perpetually living with an awareness of all that is sacred within and around you.

Choosing to be still and silent on purpose—or as I like to put it, taking a sacred pause—can be a radical, revolutionary act. In Western culture, we are taught that our worth is in being productive, constantly moving. Everybody is telling you to grind, that your effort and schedule are a reflection of your worth, but the truth is, with stillness comes knowing. There are some levels of knowing that I can't get when I'm in a frantic state of busyness, striving, trying to prove myself to the world and even to myself. It is a miracle in this culture to say I am revolutionary enough to give myself permission to sit still. People will ask, "What are you doing?" and your bold response can be "Nothing. Absolutely nothing."

Stillness and simplicity are especially radical if you are from a marginalized community. Women, Black people, Latinxs, Indigenous people, and Asians have often been treated as if our labor is our worth. Black people were literally bought and sold for our labor, productivity, and fertility. Women often note that after marriage their labor increases, while men report less stress after they get married. So if you are a part of a marginalized group and make the spiritual commitment to become unhurried, to know that even while sitting still you are already enough, already sacred, this is a life-altering awareness. In the stillness you discover chasing nothing is everything. As my grandmother would say, there are some truths, some revelations that come to us only when we sit down somewhere. Often our anxiety and insecurity keep us chasing after what we already possess.

*Imani identifies as a mixed-race Black Asian woman who has lived with anxiety and rage for much of her life. She is married and often becomes explosive toward her husband and coworkers. We began using meditation in her therapy, and I assigned it as homework for daily support. Imani quickly saw results, feeling much less anxiety and rage on the days when she meditated. She loves meditation and has now connected with a community group for meditation. While addressing the roots of her anxiety and rage was critical, she benefited from the daily spiritual practice as a way of connecting with and regulating herself. When she was able to feel less overwhelmed, we could begin to address the causes of her distress, both childhood sexual trauma and a lifetime of gendered racism.*

## GENEROSITY

When we have a stingy mentality, we are living from a place of panic, a place of "never enough." We can shift into hoarding, clinging, and over-protection instead of actually being able to open our hands and our heart and share of ourselves. Instead of seeing everyone as competitors that we have to block, beat, or outperform, we can share what we have with others.

When you begin coming home to yourself, you no longer have to frantically hold on to everything at the expense of everyone else. You no longer have to hold the view that when others lose, you win. You don't have to be mean-spirited and fight everyone. You no longer have to believe the lie that poverty is the fault of people who are impoverished, so they just need to work hard like you. You don't have to approach each day as a battle. You can release the idea that everyone needs to figure out life on their own. To come home to yourself today, what do you need to stop clinging to, hoarding, hiding, or defending? You may have been fighting for something for so long that you don't even remember why you're fighting. Consider the myths that you have believed that keep you from sharing resources, time, or love.

Being a blessing is a blessing. Sharing knowledge, mentoring, parenting, and teaching are spiritual acts. When you stop seeing everyone as a competitor, you can build real collaborations, teams, communities, families. When you no longer need to make money off everyone, you can actually see people. When you cease seeing others as winners or losers, you can actually start to love. Generosity is important to carry on your journey home. It is choosing liberation instead of confinement.

## RELEASING:
## THE ART OF SURRENDER

There is an art to realizing when and what to let go, surrender, yield, and release. I wonder if you can take a sacred pause and consider today:

- What have you been chasing that you no longer need to pursue?
- What have you been hungry and thirsty for that, in your heart of hearts, you know will not fulfill you?
- What are you willing to shift away from?
- What do you want to be the focus of your attention?

As you come home to yourself, you may need to release a job, a relationship, a mindset, or a habit. You may need to surrender old ideas about yourself. You may want to release anxiety, control, or grudges. Recognize that there are times in life when you need to release to receive. You will need to let go of some things to make room for the real thing. Let it be so. In your mind, your body, you may believe that you cannot let go. This is a spiritual matter that requires stepping out in faith and walking in the direction of a life, a way of being, that you have not previously possessed. Are you tired enough of where you have been and who you have been to walk into the liberation of truth? Let it be so. And so it is.

## SELF-COMPASSION, NOT CONDEMNATION

*Ling is a second-generation Chinese American who came to therapy with a history of unhealthy romantic relationships. She has also had numerous ruptures in her friendship circle over the years. Ling grew up feeling a lot of pressure to perform for her family and community. She struggled in school, and it left her doubting her intelligence and overcompensating for her insecurity. Many people find her defensive and argumentative. Initially in therapy, she was combative, but instead of debating with her, I would listen and try to describe things from her perspective. After several tests in which I did not take the bait to argue, Ling settled into therapy and became more open. When we eventually came to the root of her insecurities after she described several humiliating experiences at school, we were able to cultivate compassion for the child she was, the woman she became, and the condemnation she felt. As she began to have more compassion for herself, she experienced less need to overcompensate in her social interactions. She felt better about herself, and this translated into how she showed up in the world.*

We can be so hard on ourselves. We judge ourselves harshly for our feelings, our mistakes, and our journey. We are sometimes angry, disappointed, and ready to give up on ourselves. What would it look and feel like if we showed ourselves more compassion, kindness, gentleness, and acceptance?

When I run support groups and facilitate group therapy, we always set ground rules to create emotional safety in the group. These rules relate to how we're going to speak to one another and respect one another's experiences, perceptions, and values. I remind the group that we are not clones, and we don't have to be. In all my years of running these groups, I've found that what is more prevalent than people disrespecting one another is people dishonoring, condemning, and judging themselves.

To journey home entails getting to a place, spiritually, of radical self-acceptance and self-compassion, recognizing that you are a beautiful work in progress. So you can come home to yourself where you are right now. You do not have to wait until you attain unending bliss, eternal calm, or mythical perfection. You can decide to no longer beat yourself up for where you are in the process because the process is a part of the journey. When you look at your life story through the eyes of compassion, where you are now will make sense.

Often we judge ourselves harshly by comparing ourselves to other people who did not start where we started, who were not given the baggage that we are carrying, and who are not us. We have to take our gaze off other people's lanes and stay in our own. As we look at ourselves with compassion and kindness, our insight will grow, and we can better understand who we are and the choices we made at different points of our lives.

You can stop being mad at yourself for past mistakes. You didn't know then what you know now, or you didn't have the skills and support that you have now. Your past does not fully or adequately define you. What a gift it will be when you take yourself out of time-out. You can have a fulfilling life if you stop punishing yourself. I wonder if you can extend grace, acceptance, and love to yourself today. Despite all the mountains you've faced, the parts of your story that nobody else knows or that you're embarrassed about, and the ways that you've let yourself down, I wonder if you can say, "I give myself permission to turn the page from my past." When you stop condemning, judging, and punishing yourself, you can get to a place of self-compassion. Self-rejection may be blocking your journey home to yourself. As you work to psychologically navigate toward self-acceptance, you can adopt self-compassion as a spiritual value, an aspirational way of being.

## HUMILITY:
## OPENNESS TO NEW THINGS

Holistic growth, which includes spiritual growth, requires an openness to new things. In mindfulness, this is called *beginner's mind*, and according to Christian teaching, we need the open mind of a child to enter the Kingdom of Heaven. To grow into accepting the fullness of our being, we need to be curious, teachable, and open-minded. When we have a know-it-all attitude, we can never get any further than where we are right now. We have shut ourselves off from the possibility of growth, awe, or fresh revelation.

On the other hand, when you get to a place of humility, wonder, and openness, there is no limitation on how much you can grow. Walking in openness and humility is actually much easier than having to pretend to know it all. Once you adopt a posture and mindset of humility and patience, you can begin to shed the cocoon. Then you can actually see your own wings, not the fake ones that are based on pretense and that cannot take you very far. You will have the openness to enter and stay in the process of growth and development. When you slow down and are willing to recognize what you don't know, the opportunity to learn presents itself as a beautiful gift.

It is actually freeing to be able to admit to those moments in our lives when we have absolutely no idea what to do next. There are times when we might have everything planned out, but life has a way of upending our plans. Those are the times when we feel we are just along for the ride, not in the driver's seat—we have no choice but to sit back and watch the unfolding of that season. Being open to the unknown takes a level of trust. Some people trust God, some trust the universe, some trust their ancestors, some trust themselves, and some trust the process. Coming home to yourself will include some moments when you are not sure of the next step, but I hope you will remain open and patient with yourself as you continue on the journey. Anyone who works in mental health or spiritual development will tell you that you must be open in order to grow. The work of psychologists, social workers, psychiatrists, pastoral counselors, therapists, and life coaches is based on the belief that you can be more alive, fulfilled, balanced—more at home with yourself than you are right now. You may come in to therapy presenting a lot of symptoms of distress, you may have a long history of traumatic experiences, you may have suffered a lot of losses and setbacks, yet your therapist has the capacity to see for you and within you what has not yet manifested itself and then assist you in being able to see these possibilities for yourself. I invite you to adopt an openness in your spirit to the possibility that you can be at home within yourself.

*Patricia is a Caribbean American woman in her late thirties. She is very practical and organized. She decided early on, with the encouragement of her aunt, the career path she would take. She completed her education and training and has done well for herself professionally. Initially I saw Patricia as simply quiet and shy, but as time went on I began to sense there was much more to her than what she presented. After addressing her initial problem of moderate depression, Patricia began to share her dreams for the life of a spirit-led artist. She had suppressed the dreams for years because it just didn't seem practical or possible. In therapy, we began to consider the possible ways Patricia could integrate more of her spirituality and creativity into her life. The more she became open to it, the more she came alive. For the first time, I saw her laughing, speaking with more confidence, and stepping out of the box of dissatisfaction. She was on her way home.*

## SPIRITUAL AND RELIGIOUS PRACTICES

### MEDITATION

One of the practices that can help you on the journey home is meditation. There are different types of meditation. You may choose to focus on God, your breath, a word, a mantra, an image, a sensation, or a sound. Some meditations are silent, and some are guided. There are seated meditations, walking meditations, and even contemplative movement. Meditation can connect you to yourself and your Creator while it calms anxiety in your mind, franticness in your spirit, and tension in your body. You can release your agenda, petitions, and demands as you shift from striving to being. Sacred stillness and silence create an atmosphere of holiness within you and sometimes around you. Meditation, when it is connected to its spiritual roots, will affect how you show up in the world, how you treat others, and how you live your life. When you meditate only as a tool or strategy to enhance your life, you may meditate and still be mean-spirited, racist, and elitist. Meditation that is grounded in compassionate values will translate into your daily life.

## PRAYER

Prayer can be defined as communion or conversation with God, Divine Love, your Higher Power, your Source or Creator. An important aspect of prayer as conversation is that it cannot be one-sided. Many of us who come from religious traditions were taught specific things to say during prayer, including words of worship, praise, and thanksgiving, requesting forgiveness and listing petitions for yourself and others. These directives often miss a very important part, and that is silent listening, silent awareness. Prayer is not just about making requests. The very act of praying itself can be transformative. For those who practice the spiritual discipline of prayer or are open to it, I encourage you not just to center prayer on your wants but to open yourself to the refreshment and clarity that can come when you quiet your mind and are present in a sacred space. Give yourself a sacred pause to receive what you overlooked in the busyness of your day.

Both meditation throughout the day and constant prayer involve shifting our minds, hearts, and spirits consistently, instead of just devoting a few minutes to a spiritual practice each day. When we separate our sacred lives from our everyday routines, we do not allow prayer to permeate any other aspect of our lives. African psychology and other indigenous psychologies resist the false dichotomy between the sacred and secular. Not only do we pray with our mouths, but we also pray with our actions. We can approach our relationships and vocation prayerfully. Living a life of prayer can make you more aligned, in tune, and connected to yourself,

God, and others. If you pray often but are still judgmental, manipulative, or harsh, you are likely spending a lot of time talking instead of listening. As you commune with the Creator, who is Love, that same love will show up in you.

> *Elisa, a Latina day-care owner, comes from a very close-knit family that sacrificed a lot for her to have a quality education. Her uncle began struggling with substance dependence, and the entire family was engaged in trying to support his recovery. Elisa shared that her anxiety had exploded, and her insomnia was constant. We tried solutions-focused therapy, which encourages clients to use strategies that have worked for them in the past to cope with the present. Elisa disclosed that what had helped her to survive the stress and trauma of the past was prayer. She began praying more, both individually and with her family. She also prayed in therapy. As she prayed, she felt the strength to navigate her days without being overwhelmed. I encouraged her to not only pray for her uncle but also for herself, to not lose sight of herself and the impact that the family stress was having on her. With prayer, family support, and therapy, Elisa began coming home to herself.*

## FASTING

Traditional fasting is refraining from eating food. Some people fast from both food and liquids; others drink water only. Some people fast from certain foods such as sweets or meat. There are individual fasts and collective fasts where everyone in a faith community participates. Some fast breakfast and lunch and eat dinner, and others fast for the full day or several days. Fasting is an ancient practice that many cultures and faith traditions have adopted as a way of developing their spiritual awareness.

There are non-food fasts as well, with some people refraining from social media, phone calls, television, alcohol, or even dating. The idea is not just that you turn away from something, but that you turn toward nourishing your faith, your spirit. So fasting isn't the same as being on a diet. In fact, people with an eating disorder who desire to fast as a spiritual practice are encouraged to consider something besides food to refrain from. During a fast, people usually pray, meditate, and/or read holy texts. Some people give the food they would have eaten or the money they would have spent on food to someone else in need. Many people who are on a fast do not share that fact with others, because bragging and self-promotion are contrary to the purpose of fasting.

Fasting can be associated with a greater sense of clarity, a sense of connection with God, an opportunity to reorder your priorities, a way of tuning out nonsense and focusing on your spirit. You can step away from the nonsense and constant comparison of social media, you can develop a greater appreciation for the gift of food, and you can grow in your spiritual discipline rather than being controlled by substances or media. Those who are fasting with others in their spiritual or religious community will often break the fast together, which allows them to connect not only with their individual spirituality but also with their community.

## FAITH COMMUNITY

According to Christian teaching, "Iron sharpens iron" and "Deep calls to deep," so being a part of an affirming and loving faith community can encourage you to move toward spiritual development. If spiritual growth is a priority for you, it can be helpful to commune with others who share this priority. This may take the form of fasting, but it can also include meditating together, praying together, or studying sacred texts together. Some faith communities even have support groups related to important issues such as bereavement or recovery from addiction. If spirituality is important to you, connecting with others who share this value can enhance your journey home to yourself.

I encourage you to consider who is spiritually walking with you. Is your spirituality a part of yourself that you can share in your friendship circle?

Is your spiritual journey known, valued, and nourished in your romantic relationship? If you are in therapy and your faith is important to you, have you felt that you could talk about your spiritual journey with your therapist? When you have to leave parts of yourself out of the equation, it delays your journey home. I hope you can cultivate spaces where you can be your full self, including your spiritual self, whatever that looks like for you.

If you are part of a faith community, can you be your full self in that place, or do you feel pressure to pretend to be something you are not? We can't develop our spirits in places that are breaking our spirits. This is important for everyone, but especially for marginalized persons. Does your spiritual or religious community affirm and celebrate women or does it only talk about women as temptresses who need to learn to be silent? If you are a racially marginalized person, does your faith community display only White images of God, and do they fail to ever teach, preach, or engage in issues that are facing your community? Do the members of your faith community promote the idea that God is love but display hateful attitudes and use disparaging words about LGBTQ+ people? Finding spiritual or religious communities that are inclusive, welcoming, and affirming can be vital to your journey home so you can know in your spirit that you are loved and welcomed. You deserve to be in places that are nourishing, edifying, and liberating.

## JUSTICE WORK, ACTIVISM, AND EMPOWERMENT

Justice is another of the qualities that many faith traditions attribute to God, along with love. If you believe that you are to develop qualities that reflect your Creator, that means that you also value being loving and seeking justice and equity. It's amazing that some religious people will quickly argue that people of faith should focus on God, not on social justice. You have to wonder about their idea of who God is when they believe pursuing social justice is contrary to pursuing God.

Spirituality is not merely an internal experience, but it is manifested in our external actions, the fruit of what we hold inwardly. A way of expressing and cultivating our spirituality is working to make things right, advocating for the oppressed, and seeking ways to empower the marginalized. The question is not which is more important, being spiritual or making the world a better place. Rather, one leads to the other. If you value spirituality, compassion, generosity, and interconnection, this will motivate you to engage in cultivating wellness, justice, and empowerment in the world around you. When spirituality is rooted in compassion, it will move you to work toward, organize, and vote for the safety, protection, and provision of others, not just yourself.

## EXPRESSIVE ARTS

*Ruth lives with severe depression and loneliness. She has survived multiple traumas over the course of her life and had prior negative experiences in therapy. She is very vigilant and often sits in therapy holding her breath and her back tightly. Early in therapy, she disclosed that she used to be a dancer. I asked her if she was open to incorporating movement in our sessions. She agreed, and I began inviting her to use movement to breathe, to define herself, and eventually to express the unspoken traumas. When she danced, she went from blank and shut down to awakened. Sometimes she would weep, and other times she would laugh. Sometimes she would stomp in anger, and other times she would reach toward the heavens. As she began to dance her prayers for comfort and recovery, she became more peaceful. I invited Ruth to begin dancing for her therapy homework, and her movements became light posts guiding her home to herself.*

If you talk to an artist about what they have created that they consider their masterpiece, many times they will say something to the effect of "I didn't create it. It came through me. I just received it." I've heard people say this about hit songs, paintings, poems, and even choreography. Artistic expression is described by many as a spiritual experience. It is not surprising that mental health professionals have found the expressive arts to be an important pathway for healing, connection, and growth. I have seen the way the arts can awaken people on a deep level, whether they're children or adults making collages, playing instruments, or role playing. When we are not creating art to impress or to sell but to express what is within us, it can facilitate the journey home to ourselves. This includes storytelling, writing raps, and creating crafts. When you approach the arts from a place of openness and allow yourself to clearly express your feelings without fear, your spirit and the spirits of those who witness it can be touched in beautiful ways.

## HOMEWORK

I invite you to read the following blessing aloud as often as you like. If it does not resonate with you, feel free to write one that aligns with your spirit and then read it aloud as often as you like.

*I am blessed from the top of my head to the soles of my feet.*
*I receive peace in my spirit, heart, mind, and body.*
*I apply loving-kindness to my wounds and my memories.*
*I am fully aware that I am not alone in this journey called life.*
*I open myself to love, including love for myself.*
*I allow truth to show up and liberate me from the limitation of lies I*
   *have been told about myself.*
*I tell myself the truth.*
*I am learning to be more compassionate, present, open, generous,*
   *connected, and willing to release what I no longer need.*
*My soul tells my heart, mind, body, and spirit, "Welcome home."*

# PART THREE

Recovering from Roadblocks
on the Journey Home

# CHAPTER NINE

# Mourning Invisible Losses

*When I was growing up, my mother introduced me to poetry. I memorized incredible poems and participated in dramatic reading contests. I also began writing poetry and sharing it at coffeehouses and other venues. Eventually, I learned about poetry slams, competitions where people share their spoken word artistry. When I lived in Boston, I worked with a gifted community of spoken word artists and regularly put on shows that incorporated spoken word, music, dance, and visual art. As I grew older, I immersed myself in my career and family life and had less and less time for poetry. Actually, I should say I made less and less time for poetry. One night after my children went to sleep, I went online and began listening to different poets. I was startled when the tears came down my face. It was more than missing writing and performing; I missed me. There is a part of me that comes alive in poetry, and I had to reclaim that. I had to reclaim me.*

invite you to get into a comfortable position and begin to focus in on your breath. As you come home to yourself, you become more aware of the ways you have distracted yourself from the pain with extreme productivity, loud voices, nonstop television watching, addictive phone scrolling, steady sipping, and late-night eating until you fall asleep. You shift away from the constant busyness used to cover the pain. To come home is to stop running away from your grief.

This grief in the pit of your stomach, the base of your back, the side of your head, the back of your throat, the core of your heart—you cannot ignore your grief. Eventually it makes its presence known. It will not be denied.

The journey back to yourself requires you to acknowledge the people and things that you lost, that were taken, and that you gave away. The losses may have occurred during your season of disconnection from yourself, when you were wandering around looking for home in all the wrong places, or the losses may be the cause of your disconnection. These losses are a painful reality, but to complete the journey home, you have to see them clearly.

Acknowledging your losses may help motivate you to continue the journey back to yourself. When you get to the place where you have given up so much or have had so much taken, you recognize that disconnection is not worth it. It has numbed you, but it has not saved you. As you look at your losses and the sacredness of your time and life, you are no longer willing to exchange yourself, your values, your integrity, your safety, or your mental health for anything that promised relief from the grief but did not deliver. Money, popularity, or whatever is being offered is not worth what you have sacrificed for it.

You get to that place Fannie Lou Hamer, the Black American civil rights and women's rights activist, described as being sick and tired of being sick and tired. Perhaps you need to ask yourself if you are tired of running, tired of numbing, or tired of denying. The decision to face your grief is yours alone to make. You may have had other people try to tell you that you need to grieve, but if you were not ready, you did not hear it, believe it, or act on it. You may have gotten mad at them, ignored them, or disconnected from them because you did not want to hear their call to grieve.

Nobody else can tell you when you've had enough striving, straining, or self-destructing to avoid grieving what you have lost and what you continue to lose. One of the painful things that I had to discover is that when you have a history of trauma, you often have a high tolerance for emotional pain. You've had to learn to endure, persevere, and hold the pain in. Some of you even learned how to do it with grace, with gloss, without the slightest hint that you have been affected by losses. People may interact with you and have no idea of the pain or heartbreak you carry. You wear your mask so well that your homecoming may not be because you can't fake it anymore, but because you choose not to. I'm glad you've reached this important milestone on the journey home. You could have spent the remainder of your life living as a fraction of the person you are, but you chose not to.

For others, you did not choose this time, but the time chose you. The mask cracked, and the river of grief erupted and would not be denied. You may have hit rock bottom and couldn't take it anymore. You may have experienced a steady boil that intensified over time, until you woke up and said to yourself, "I better get out of this pot before it destroys me." You may not know what grieving looks like for you, but you do know you were not created to live in the margins of your heart anymore.

## RECOGNIZE THE LOSSES

*Faith is an Asian American international student who came to the States for graduate school. She was excited and had researched the program extensively online. She even looked up the city and found a place to live before she came. Her family was excited for her, and her friends told her how lucky she was, so she was not prepared for the losses. At first she didn't even know how to name them. She missed speaking her language everywhere she went. She missed fitting in without question. She missed being*

*called by her birth name, even though she was the one who de-
cided to go by Faith in the States. She missed food, music, sights,
and the simple fun of sitting around with family and friends eating, laughing, and talking. She missed not having to repeat herself or not understanding cultural references people regularly
made in classes or social circles. She missed home. She came to
therapy to grieve and to figure out a way to be at home within
herself while so far from her actual home. A part of her journey
included connecting with other international students and then
people in the larger community from her home country. A part of
the journey also included responding to discrimination and releasing shame for being different.*

Consider what you lost during your season(s) of disconnection. You've lost
time as you lived someone else's life, trying to be something you're not or
chasing what wasn't for you. You may have lost hope, which led you to
settle because you no longer believed, or perhaps never believed, you could
have good things in life. Additionally, you may have lost your faith—your
belief in God, yourself, or other people.

Remember when you used to believe in the full possibilities of life instead of your current temporary circumstances? As time passed, bitterness
may have taken over, so not only did you give up on your dreams, but you
also shot down other dreamers, assuming you were protecting them from
disappointment. You may have adjusted to a deflated, confined view of
reality and lost some dreams and hopes along the way.

## RELATIONSHIP LOSSES

*Antoinette, a young Deaf White woman, numbed the pain of
childhood abuse with addiction. While using and abusing sub-*

*stances, she mistreated and lied to many family members and friends. As she worked on her sobriety, she began to see the deep wounds that she had caused, manifesting in the fact that many people didn't trust her or want to be around her. She had to grieve those losses and take responsibility for the ways she had created or deepened those disconnections. Some people were willing to work with her on rebuilding the relationship and were supportive of her recovery. Others were unwilling to believe that she could be different, and she had to grieve that those relationships were irreparable, at least in this current season.*

During seasons of disconnection, you may have lost your confidence, so you no longer advocate for yourself. You may have gotten to the place of accepting anything. You may be surprised by some of the circumstances you tolerated and dysfunction you accommodated. When you have lost sight of yourself, you can unknowingly allow your wounds to make decisions for you. When you're wounded, it is hard to take care of yourself, let alone maintain friendships and romantic relationships.

You may have lowered your standards and released all expectations after losing faith in relationships and yourself. Remember when you used to think real friends would consistently treat you with love, esteem, and honesty? Remember when you used to think that a relationship with someone who honored you was possible? Remember the time before you started believing everyone was terrible, so you might as well hold on to the terrible you know?

## HEALTH LOSSES

*Amelia, a forty-three-year-old Black woman, has faced a lot of pain, bullying, and discrimination based on her size. She has struggled with her relationship with food her whole life. She grew up in a home with one parent who was emotionally volatile and another who was emotionally shut down. There was not a lot of verbal affirmation or extra money for gifts, but her parents expressed their care with food and shelter. As an adult, Amelia feels the most loved or cared for when eating and shopping. While people can be healthy at a range of sizes, Amelia's health has suffered: she has high blood pressure, type 2 diabetes, and sleep apnea. Her shopping has also created a lot of debt, which contributed to her depression and anxiety. Her homecoming included grieving the emotional losses of her childhood, creating healthy relationships and coping strategies in her present, and healing her relationship with her body to replace shame with self-love.*

In seasons when you lost connection with yourself, you may have also lost your sleep, appetite, and health. Stress shows up in your body—even if you say you're fine, your body tells a different story. Your body was not designed to live in a constant state of vigilance. Your body was created to respond to crisis and then return to balance. When you have lived with constant stress and danger, your body pays a price.

## PROFESSIONAL LOSSES

Disconnection from yourself can also lead to financial losses because you are not operating from a place of wisdom or clarity. You may have begun performing below your ability because there was so much weighing you down. Try not to judge yourself harshly for the opportunities, money, or positions you lost when you lost sight of yourself.

I have worked with victims of sexual harassment, and they are often people who had performed well at their jobs until the harassment started.

As a result of the harassment, they started coming in late, missing more days, and being anxious and distracted. They couldn't focus because they were constantly looking out for the perpetrator. Their work suffered, and then the same supervisor who harassed them would write them up and say they weren't functioning at the expected level.

Examine the times when you were forced to disconnect from yourself and think about how that affected your education and work trajectory. Some teachers or supervisors may have described you as being all over the place while you were trying so hard to forget painful memories and losses. Even those of you who have been successful can show a greater appreciation for all that you accomplished in the midst of trauma. If you did not have to expend all that energy fighting through the cobwebs of your past and present, you could have devoted more energy to your dreams, hopes, joy, and love.

## MENTAL HEALTH LOSSES

*Kareem was diagnosed with bipolar disorder in his early twenties. While the diagnosis and subsequent treatment and medication brought some relief, there were also losses he and his family had to grieve. He had to grieve the false belief that his challenges were temporary and could be managed by willpower and determination alone. He had to grieve the consequences he was left to face because of his depressive episodes. He had to grieve the harmful things he did when he was manic. He had to grieve the fact that some people who saw him when he was not taking medication were now afraid of him. He had to grieve the stigma that made him afraid to tell new friends and potential dating partners about his diagnosis. He had to grieve the lost connection to family members who did not "believe in mental illness" and told him he just needed to get right with God. We created space to grieve and also began to reimagine the life he wanted to build.*

Give yourself space and permission to mourn the losses you've experienced not only in your physical health and professional life but also in your psychological wellness. Being disconnected from yourself can deepen depression. It may have made you more anxious or insecure or made it more difficult to trust yourself and others. Psychological homelessness is a sense of being emotionally lost or disconnected from yourself. For some of you, the sense of psychological homelessness may have led to suicidal thoughts because you wished you could escape your life or pain. Consider the methods you used in the past or present to medicate your pain: puffs, penetration, pastries, or something else.

## SPIRITUAL LOSSES

You have spiritual gifts and spiritual purpose in your life. However, when you're disconnected from yourself, it may be difficult to see your gifts, connect with a sense of meaning, or engage in a regular spiritual practice. When you feel spiritually lost, the idea of being spiritually at home within yourself may seem unattainable. You may see others on spiritual journeys that sound fulfilling, but you may never have experienced what they describe, or it was such a distant part of your past that you no longer feel connected to it. You may have attended spiritual or religious services, workshops, conferences, or retreats and saw everyone else engaged, connected, and fortified, while you came away feeling nothing. This may have been because you were daydreaming about what you were going to do later, observing what everyone else was doing, or critiquing the experience. All of these are barriers to being at home within your spirit. To come home to your spirit is to risk the vulnerability of being present without the distraction of monitoring and critiquing other people. The spiritual home-coming is an openness to what is happening within you, awakening the parts of yourself that are beyond fear, trauma, judgment, or social pressure. There may have been times in your life when there was so much going on that it was hard to focus on breath, God, faith, or hope. In the absence of self-compassion and grace, and in the presence of negative self-talk or condemning community messages, you may have blamed and shamed yourself for your spiritual struggles. As you consider your spiritual losses and your experiences of disconnection, judgment, confusion, shame, and powerlessness, grieve.

Healing requires truth-telling. There are times when others want you to hurry up and get over your pain because they're uncomfortable with your grief. If you are honest, you'll admit there have been times when you couldn't or chose not to sit with your pain, so you tried to convince yourself that you were over it. As you come home to yourself, make the decision to hold space in your heart to grieve the things and people you lost during your seasons of disconnection.

Toxic spirituality has silenced many of us. Messages like "Just be grate-ful because others have it worse" or "Just look on the bright side and count your blessings" lack compassion. Homecoming means we don't need the Trauma Olympics of deciding who has it worse. Your grief over your losses is significant; at least allow it to be significant for you. For example, during the COVID-19 pandemic, some essential workers shared their distress about the risk of contamination, while others responded by saying, "You should be grateful you have a job." This type of shaming and silencing is not healing or helpful. Another example is when people try to give things toxic spiritual meaning. I had a client who was molested, and her minister told her the molestation by her father was a test from God to see if she really loves God or if she will surrender her faith. Lack of compassion, ac-countability, and caregiving by people who claim to be spiritual or religious can lead to further losses for those on the homecoming journey. Let me say clearly that misguided or even hateful people who have some sort of spiritual authority do not have the final say in your spiritual journey home to yourself. People who reveal themselves to be harmful to your wellness, safety, and spirit are roadblocks on the journey home. You will need to walk around them to reclaim your spirit, mind, heart, and body.

## MOURNER'S BENCH:
## AN INVITATION TO GRIEVE

While I am not physically with you, I am emotionally and spiritually with you. There is also a community built around *The Homecoming Podcast* and this book standing in solidarity with you and cheering for our collective journey home. Alongside this great cloud of witnesses, I encourage you to give yourself full permission to acknowledge the pain, regret, and losses. At this altar or mourner's bench there is room for all the ways your grief shows up, as long as you are not harming yourself or others. It may show up in crying, praying, trembling, rocking, sighing, tightening your muscles, shallow breathing, or screaming. You may feel the desire to take a break from this chapter, and if you do, that is fine as well. The rest of this chapter will be here waiting for you when you return. Just know that taking a break is different from running from the truth, which is exhausting and ultimately ineffective. So when you are ready to face it, you can continue the journey.

You may want to pour your grief out on a canvas or in your journal. You may want to sing or dance it. You may want to massage your neck and back or begin taking cleansing breaths. You may also just want to sit and see it, sit and feel it. As you sit with your losses, you discover that you can acknowledge them, feel the grief and not be drowned by it. You can feel and still breathe or regain your breath. As you sit with your unacknowledged losses, you can begin to tell yourself the truth about the hurt, disappointment, anger, sadness, or guilt.

The truth may be that you don't like the current state of your life, regardless of what others may think. You may be aware that you are no-where near where you wanted to be at this age. The point of telling yourself the truth is not to feel bad about it, but to motivate you to change the aspects of your life that you want to revise, rebuild, release, or reclaim. The losses of life can motivate you to get back home to yourself. To reclaim your life, time, health, dreams, and voice.

*Blessed are those who mourn, for they shall be comforted.*
—MATTHEW 5:4

Identify the losses you want to reclaim. Perhaps you want to reclaim your acceptance of your body, your prayer life, your comfort with affection, your neglected friendships, your educational goals, or even your self-confidence. When you renew your clarity and decide to no longer hide in confusion, you accelerate the journey home. There are times when you knew what you wanted, felt, or thought, but your self-doubt was so all-consuming that it was easier to hide in confusion because it gave you permission not to act. You can take a step forward in this moment by ac-knowledging, "I'm not confused about what I feel, think, or want. I'm afraid." There are some things you already know, so you don't have to keep polling more people, looking for permission from your therapist, minister, friends, or family members.

You have inner wisdom. There is a Swahili word, *kujua*, which gener-ally means to know, but some translate this word as "remembering that which I already know." In this moment, activate the wisdom and knowl-edge that's already in you, so you don't have to cling to confusion anymore. You can at least acknowledge that "I know but I'm not ready." (You might not be ready to say the truth out loud, or to let go of certain people or sea-sons, or to walk in the direction of your dreams.) You may want to ac-knowledge in this moment that you're not sure of the way forward, but you know that where you are now is not where you want to stay, whether that place is physical, spiritual, psychological, social, or vocational.

While there are some losses you can reclaim or rebuild, you must acknowledge the people and things that are permanently gone and are not coming back. If you lost time doing things or being with people who drained you more than they edified you, you can grieve this while also seeing any ways in which that time was not a total loss. You can also grieve the people that you cannot get back because of death, divorce, or other ruptures in the relationship.

While you grieve these losses, be open to new sources of hope, or even hope for the return of what you lost. Your parent may have died, abandoned you, or not shown up for you emotionally, but you can meet new people who parent you, mentor you, protect you, advocate for you, or nurture you. The divorce may be final, but down the road if you are open to it, new love may be available to you. You may have failed miserably at that exam, but there may be opportunities to try again in another class or in another year. You may have lost the opportunity to work with one person who could have helped you professionally, but you may meet others who will open future doors for you. You may have suffered miscarriage or infertility, but you have found some joy in blessing other children who enter your life in various ways.

You reclaim the losses you can, and you open yourself to new manifestations of joy. This is not about replacing people because people cannot be replaced, but it is about experiencing losses and still living a whole life.

Grieving and reclaiming is a continuous process because we're always growing, changing, and evolving. So get yourself back. Get your music, poems, dance, and even your appetite back.

*One day when I was home from college, a dear friend of mine was over at my house and she was upset about a breakup. My mom made dinner, and my friend said she didn't want to eat because she was upset about this breakup. My mom said, "Don't you ever let a man take your money or your appetite; you better come to this table and eat this food."*

I don't know what has been taken from you, but I do know that there is a whole wide world that is still available to you. Most important, you need to become available to yourself. Will you open yourself to receive? Will you open your heart, mind, and spirit to no longer live shut down? Will you awaken to the truth articulated by Fannie Lou Hamer, that as you look at the pervasiveness of trauma and oppression "you're sick and tired of being sick and tired"?

At times, you may have been your own worst enemy. Other times, however, you may have encountered perpetrators, abusers, racists, violators, enemies who intentionally took things from you. So whether you gave away parts of yourself or they were stolen from you, I invite you to reclaim what you can.

Make the decision to no longer wear the costume and recite the lines that others want to see and hear. As you journey home, take the script that has been handed to you and return it to the sender. You will begin to have the confidence to recognize and say when something is not for you.

## HOMEWORK

I invite you to choose one thing that you're going to get back. It may be something you can get back today, or it may take years. You may want to reclaim your rest and commit to going to bed earlier, or you may want to reclaim your education and go back to school. You may want to reclaim your physical health and commit to exercising and eating more nourishing foods, or you may want to reclaim your mental health and commit to therapy. Some of you may have lost your children because of an addiction or an abusive relationship. If it is possible for you to go take classes and access resources to have more stability in your life so you can reclaim your children, consider taking those steps. You may have lost touch with your children during a divorce but want to reclaim or rebuild relationships with them now if that is possible. You may have lost a relationship due to an unwillingness to apologize and make amends. Perhaps today is the day you want to make that call. You may have lost your confidence to try new things, and today is the day you consider applying for a new job, reentering the dating world, or looking for a new faith community. You may have lost your ability to say no, but starting today, you commit to protecting your time, energy, and mental health by being more selective with your yeses.

If the following words align with you, reading them aloud may plant them in your heart:

*I will no longer entertain anything that requires me to be something I am not.*

*I make a radical, revolutionary decision to come for what's mine, and nothing is going to keep me from me.*

*May it be so, and so it is.*

Today, as you tell yourself the truth about your losses and give yourself permission to grieve, I invite you to reclaim yourself by allowing your soul to tell your heart, mind, body, and spirit, "Welcome home."

# CHAPTER TEN

# Healing from Breakups and Divorce

*A number of years ago I was leading a women's group at a local church. At the end of one meeting a woman approached me nervously. She shared that she really enjoyed it but wanted to check with me to make sure it was okay for her to be there. I was puzzled and asked her to explain what she meant. She shared that she had gone through a divorce recently, and because of it she was rejected by her old church. It saddened me that a woman who was heartbroken had been turned away from a place that is supposed to be a sanctuary. Many times, when people experience heartbreak, they find it hard to get help on the journey back home to themselves.*

When you have had a relationship come to an end, it can disrupt your sense of self. Oftentimes, even in the midst of the relationship, you may have already begun losing yourself because you have been trying so hard to hold on to someone. Whatever the depth of the relationship—whether it lasted weeks, months, or years; whether it ended in a divorce, a separation, or a breakup—I want you to know that your heart matters and your heartbreak matters. I invite you to create a safe place for yourself, a sanctuary where you don't have to try to hold it together. Create space where you don't have to convince your former partner, other people, or even yourself that you're fine.

Give yourself a safe place where you can be honest with yourself about the heartbreak, disappointment, sadness, grief, anger, or confusion. Give yourself permission to be honest about those feelings of desperation, humiliation, loneliness, shock, and for some of you . . . relief. The reality is that you can experience more than one of those feelings at the same time. You may be anxious and angry or relieved and sad. Those emotions can coexist, so the first step toward healing after a breakup is to come out of denial. The truth is, it's over; if it feels right, you may just want to whisper that to yourself: "It's over. It's over."

Some of you have been holding your breath, waiting. You may have been waiting for the other person to change their mind and choose you. You may even be the one who decided to end it, but you are still in shock about being alone again or about the way it ended. The situation may not seem real to you, because when you put your trust in a person, a relationship, or a marriage, you had certain assumptions or expectations that were not met. You may have felt fairly or absolutely certain that the relationship would last, so when the rug was pulled from under you, it stunned you. You may feel let down by yourself, by the other person, by love, or even by God (those of you who prayed for things to be different). While you may not have imagined you would be alone at this point in your life, the truth is that the relationship is really over, and it's time to heal and begin again.

## SITTING WITH YOUR FEELINGS

*José, a Latino father of three, never expected his interracial marriage to end in his fifties. After weathering the storms of rejection*

*from their families in their early years, he and his wife got stuck
in a cycle where he was emotionally shut down and she was angry,
and they would continue to trigger each other. The more emotionally unavailable he was, the angrier she became, and the angrier
she became, the more he shut down. His wife wanted a divorce, but
José prayed for God to save their marriage. It didn't happen. Years
later he is still in shock and mourning, grieving his vision of what
his marriage was supposed to be and feeling rejected by God for
not answering his prayers. He came to therapy in need of a homecoming, to grieve not only the loss of his marriage and faith but
also the early loss of his childhood best friend to cancer, and to
explore his ideas about himself, intimacy, and God.*

As you acknowledge the end of a relationship, it is important that you begin to sit with and accept what you feel without judgment. Release the pressure of what your friends, your family, or even your ex say you should feel. Those people are not you, so you don't need their approval, agreement, or permission to feel what you feel. Even if you are coming out of an unhealthy relationship, a part of you might still miss the person. Why would you miss someone who didn't treat you well? You had history together, you were connected in some ways, there were some good moments, and they may have treated you better than others have in the past. On the other hand, even if the person was very kind but you were not fulfilled in the relationship, you may feel relieved yet guilty for ending it. Tell yourself the truth about what you feel, as layered or complicated as it may be. Give yourself the gift of honesty because you cannot heal what you will not acknowledge.

Give yourself space and time to grieve, to reflect, and to heal. Healing and feeling do not need to be rapid-fire. You do not need to cry once, send them a million text messages, and declare you're all better now. Your emotions may have erupted in a moment, but the healing work takes time and space. Do not run from it or rush it by busying yourself with work, burying yourself in sleep, or burdening yourself with endless distractions.

# CHOOSE YOU:
# AFFIRM YOUR WORTH

*Lisa, a thirty-six-year-old Asian woman, lived with her boyfriend for over a decade, hoping that he would marry her. He shared early on his reservations about marriage, but she hoped that with love and patience he would change his mind. By the end of their relationship, there was no communication and only occasional sex. Lisa eventually ended it formally but felt her long-term partner had ended it by refusing to marry her. She felt devastated that she had given so many years of her life to a relationship that did not end with the family life she desired. She also felt unworthy and insecure about having given what she felt was her best—not perfection, but consistent effort over time—and that having not been enough. Her pain intensified when a year later, her ex became engaged to the person he'd started dating after he and Lisa had broken up. Lisa had to shift her focus from her ex-boyfriend and his fiancée and begin to heal and rebuild herself. Her journey home could not be delayed by waiting for her ex-boyfriend to affirm her worth.*

You are valuable and worthy of love. Breakups can really break you: your heart, your confidence, your self-esteem. If your partner's affirmation in loving and choosing you built you up, their absence can break you down. This can be devastating, especially if this relationship was central to your idea of who you are. If your partner was your home base, your mirror, your foundation, and your identity, the devastation may feel intolerable. You will need to choose and affirm yourself to come home to freedom. Self-affirmation will be more sustainable and healing then jumping into a rebound relationship, looking for approval from others without ever healing and approving of yourself. It is true that a part of healing is relational and takes place in connection with others, but it is also true that an aspect of healing is internal—psychological, spiritual, physical, and emotional. I invite you to choose you before you choose another, and to love yourself rather than look for love in all the wrong places. I invite you to heal and affirm yourself before you go out in the world, hungry for compliments and thirsty to be seen. Dare to believe that your value and love for yourself are not dependent on someone else believing in it.

Remember to appreciate your identity beyond being someone else's boo, boyfriend, girlfriend, wife, partner, husband, fiancé, or fiancée. You are more than those labels and identities. Coming home to yourself in the aftermath of heartbreak requires getting reacquainted with yourself and appreciating yourself.

## LEARN FROM YOUR RELATIONSHIP

As you tend to the wounds at the end of a relationship, do not overlook the opportunity to learn from it.

- What did you learn about yourself?
- What did you learn about your needs and wants?
- What did you learn about communication?
- What did you learn about who and what you find attractive?
- What did you learn about grace, compassion, and forgiveness of yourself and others?
- What did you learn about intimacy and connection?
- What did you learn about love?
- What warning signs did you discover?
- What and who did you discover is healing for you?

Oftentimes at the end of a relationship, we will declare that there was no way we could have seen the end coming. In some cases, this is true, but in many cases, it is not. I encourage you to look back over the early stages of the relationship and see if there were things you noticed but didn't think were a big deal. Sometimes we ignore warning signs, hoping or assuming the other person will change with time. The purpose of looking back is not to blame or shame yourself but to give you wisdom and knowledge as you go forward with your life.

Some things we do not know to look for until we have the life experience that reveals to us that they are important. Perhaps in the aftermath you learned that it is important for you and your partner to have similar approaches to financial planning, parenting, faith, alone time, time with friends, conflict, politics, substance use, or fidelity. Sometimes we fall in love with a person's potential instead of who they are at this moment.

Not only do we learn about the person and the relationship, but we also learn about ourselves. Consider if there are unhealed wounds that you had before you even met this person, and how those wounds may have contributed to your choosing them or to how you showed up in the relationship. Wounds from childhood and past relationships can affect your expectations, assumptions, and responses and can set you up for unfulfilling relational dynamics. As you prioritize healing your broken heart, you may want to consider addressing other heartbreaking experiences that have affected you. Mistreatment in your past can make you more inclined to accept or ignore continued mistreatment. It is important for you not to blame yourself because no one deserves mistreatment. It can also be helpful to acknowledge past experiences that may have caused you to think love means endurance and tolerance, no matter what. A breakup can give us an opportunity to unlearn and relearn the ways in which we want to experience, give, and receive love.

If you were the one to break someone else's heart, it is important to examine ways that you may have sabotaged the relationship as a result of unaddressed wounds. Consider the way you spoke to and treated the person and handled the issues that arose. We can learn from both what was done to us and what we did to others. By learning from the past, we are in a better place to heal and make different choices in the future. If, however, you are escaping from an abusive relationship, do *not* take responsibility for the abuse. You did not deserve it, and there is no justification for it.

Regardless of how the relationship ended, give yourself space for reflection, honesty, and humility in telling yourself the truth about what happened within you and between you and your partner. Truth and knowledge can guide us back home to ourselves.

## NOURISHING CONNECTIONS

*Monique, a Black nurse in her late thirties, was shocked when her wife of nine years had an affair. Her wife disclosed it after realizing she had acquired a sexually transmitted infection. Monique was brokenhearted and speechless. As she went through the divorce proceedings, she found that no one in her friendship circle could relate. They had either never married or were still married. Monique found sacred space in a support group for people who were separated or divorced. In the weekly group meetings, she appreciated being able to listen and gain insight from other people's experiences, to share her story without fear of judgment, and to learn healthy ways of coping from the facilitators.*

As you heal, cultivate and nourish positive friendships. Sometimes when we isolate ourselves, we can replay in our minds a distorted script, which psychologists describe as cognitive distortion. If we don't have someone to bounce ideas off of, sometimes we'll keep telling ourselves things that aren't true. Being with good friends who can be honest and caring can help us navigate the journey home.

I also encourage you to consider therapy so you can talk to someone who does not have an agenda and who can try to hear things from an unbiased perspective. Therapy can be a place of reflection, growth, and healing. You do not have to defend yourself or overexplain yourself. Some weeks you may need more silence, and other weeks you may need to express your sorrow or anger. Wherever you are is acceptable, as the therapeutic space is for you.

If you are spending all of your time by yourself, it can magnify your sense of loneliness, which can sometimes lead to going back to a situation that is not good for you. Spending time with positive people, family, friends, and therapists can help you tolerate this uncomfortable season of your life. Nourishing people do not require you to be fake. You don't need to demonstrate fake joy, fake energy, fake anything. In their presence, you can be all of what you are in the moment, even if that is empty. These are the people that you can sit with in silence, or cry, rant, and even give voice to the parts of your story you have not shared with anyone else yet. They are not people for whom you have to pretend or perform, and they won't break your confidence by sharing your secrets or ridiculing you. Good connections remind you who you are beyond the relationship you had with your ex, and with the support of these friends and family members, you can make the journey to reclaim and even re-create yourself.

## TAKE SPACE

Unless you are co-parenting with your former partner, I invite you to really think about reducing communication and interaction, at least while you're still feeling raw in the immediate aftermath of the relationship. Even those who are co-parenting will need to establish some boundaries about when, how, and what you communicate. Everyone's needs are different, so I will not offer specifics on how to set those boundaries, but I invite you to recognize the huge shift in your relationship. Sometimes people want to jump into being friends right away, without giving themselves time to grieve, heal, or process the end of the relationship. This can lead to confusion, further harm, and extended grief. Additionally, many people were not friends before the relationship, so trying to reclaim something that never existed can create more problems. If you do decide to remain friends, be sure your ex is treating you the way a true friend should.

Taking space for a season can give both you and your ex time for clarity and insight. You may want your ex to answer questions about their actions in the relationship, but if they have not yet healed or reflected, they might not have the answers you're looking for. You may believe that you need the answers in order to heal, but often in the midst of a breakup, your ex is not in a place to engage with you in a fruitful way. Demanding answers from an unaware, desperate, angry, or hurt person can create more pain. When people talk out of their wounds and their defensiveness, without self-reflection, very little healing can take place for either person.

Consider the way you need to create space for your healing and clarity. This may mean unfollowing your ex on social media, not contacting them by phone, not meeting in person, and telling mutual friends not to give you updates on their life. Give yourself breathing room, emotionally and physically.

Cultivate your other friendships and also learn how to appreciate solitude. You don't constantly have to have someone in your space. You can come home to you and actually enjoy the gift of silence. Spending time with yourself is not a punishment. It can be painful not to have someone to come home to or to share your day with, but you are a gift, and being present with yourself is also a gift. There undoubtedly were painful, unfulfilling, or difficult moments in the relationship. Now you have some space without the tension. Occupy it. Occupy your life, your body, your heart, your mind, and your spirit.

Depending on your circumstances, your ex doesn't necessarily need to stay out of your life forever. Just give yourself space and time for growth, insight, and healing. Move forward when you are free of baggage.

## ENDING EMOTIONAL ENTANGLEMENT

*Jonathon's wife filed for divorce, which was finalized two years ago. He was shocked and embarrassed, even though he realized his infidelity was the primary cause. Jonathan's ex-wife said they could be friends, but his friends watched with concern as he continued to hope to reconcile with her. He would drop everything whenever she called, purchase extravagant gifts that she not so subtly requested, and suffer in silence as she began dating other people. Jonathan's life was on hold. He ignored the warnings of friends that he was being used. Eventually he came to therapy after having a panic attack because of an exchange with his ex. Jonathan had to acknowledge and grieve the ending of the marriage, which also meant he needed to stop being emotionally invested in the relationship.*

After a breakup, you will need to release any investment you have in your ex's opinion of you. If you have done harm, you may want to confess, apologize, and even atone for it. Once you have addressed the harm, however, you cannot and should not live your life perpetually looking back. Your ex may not forgive you, but you have to live with those consequences, whether fair or not. Some people may think poorly of you because of what you have actually done, or because of the version of the story they have heard from your ex. It is usually not beneficial to go around trying to convince people of your narrative. This can create more stress and conflict, delaying your healing. When you and your partner have very different viewpoints about what happened, it can be helpful to process both your perception of the experience and any truth that may reside in their perception. This requires space, maturity, and openness. Make peace with yourself and with people who are able to offer support and insight.

It is also important to release the need to investigate everything that went down in the relationship. Trying to track down everything your ex ever did verbally, sexually, or otherwise can be a never-ending, unfulfilling mission. You can give yourself permission to say you know enough. Further details will likely not change anything for the better, and can actually make you feel worse. Sometimes people talk themselves into circles trying to figure out if their ex ever loved them. This can be a pointless, endless discussion. I encourage you to re-center yourself around your healing and your new beginning. You owe it to yourself to come home.

## ENDING SEXUAL ENTANGLEMENT

Sexual disentanglement requires telling yourself the truth that you cannot care deeply for someone one week and the next week say that you are going to have sex with them with no strings attached. Meaningless sex with someone you recently had a meaningful relationship with does not work. If you deceive yourself about the feelings involved, it can lead to further hurt for you or your former partner. Often one of you will be hoping to rekindle the relationship.

In addition to releasing physical involvement with your ex, you may also need to release any negative ways the relationship may have affected your body image, your comfort with intimacy, or your confidence in expressing yourself sexually. You may be holding on to their criticism or rejection of you. Instead of evaluating yourself based on their words or who they are now with, write a new script—a love song to yourself. Begin to compliment and affirm yourself. Your ex does not get to have the final say on your beauty, attractiveness, or sexuality. It is up to you to revise your perception of yourself.

## ADDITIONAL ENTANGLEMENTS

If you are no longer in a relationship, you should do everything you can to financially detach from your ex. This of course does not include alimony, child support, and those types of commitments. Remaining financially entangled can stall your healing. Be careful that money is not being used to control you, manipulate you, or mandate continued access. When there are ongoing financial arrangements, try to keep the communication around them minimal, respectful, and honest.

A final area of disengagement is spiritual. We connect spiritually with people we invest time, energy, and love in. If this resonates with you, I invite you to put one hand on your heart and one hand on your abdomen and reflect on your breath. Breathe at your own pace. I invite you to visualize your former partner. See them clearly and repeat the following words if they feel right to you. (If the words don't align, you may say what feels true in your heart, mind, body, and spirit.)

*I release you.*
*I release you from my emotions.*
*I release you from my heart.*
*I release you from my mind.*
*I release you from my body.*
*I release you from my spirit.*

Take a sacred pause to reflect on this release.

Healing is not only psychological and spiritual, but also physical. As an act of embodied healing, I invite you, whether standing or sitting, to begin physically dusting yourself off. Consider any thought, word, or action from the relationship that has left a heaviness on you, and use your hands to dust off your face, your neck, your shoulders, and your entire body. As you dust off, remember to breathe.

## HOMEWORK

-------------------------------------------------------------------

Once a day for the next week, I invite you to place one hand on your head and one hand on your heart, and picture yourself. See your face looking back at you and repeat the following words (or others that resonate with you).

> *I choose you.*
> *You are worthy of love.*
> *You are worthy of grace.*
> *You are worthy of compassion.*
> *I choose you.*

You can now take a cleansing breath as you remove your hands.

I invite your soul to tell your heart, mind, body, and spirit, "Welcome home."

# CHAPTER ELEVEN

# Coping and Healing from a Toxic Workplace

*I worked in a toxic environment for a few years, and it was draining—emotionally, physically, and spiritually. A coworker friend was a saving grace for me in that place. We would talk, pray, and plan together as we tried to navigate those difficult waters. My friend's outlet for her distress involved perpetually reorganizing and cleaning her office, while my distress manifested in the growing stacks of paper on my desk. In meetings when things went off the rails, it was a blessing to know she was in the room, and eventually we left the job around the same time. The gifts of that place include the work I was able to do, the ongoing friendships that started there, and a greater appreciation for subsequent work situations that put me much more at ease.*

encourage you to think about times when you have been in a psychologically harmful and draining work environment. Some of you may not have to think too far back because you may currently work at such a place. Spending a lot of time in these spaces can cause you to disconnect from yourself. You will need to heal and reconnect so you can authentically and freely move forward in the ways that really strengthen your gifts and fulfill your calling.

You can begin to reconnect with yourself by telling yourself the truth. Working in that job, at that place, and with those people has had an impact on your mental health. You may be used to the script of always claiming that you're fine, or you may gloss over the stress by focusing on gratitude—for being able to pay your bills, for example. As you continue to journey home to yourself, I invite you to tell yourself the truth about how the work environment drained you, shook your confidence, and caused you to dilute your dreams and downgrade your value. Be honest about how you might have gotten caught up in pettiness and nonsense, or been distracted by conflicts not aligned with your purpose. I invite you to be honest about jobs where your contribution, intelligence, and gifts were overlooked or even undermined.

## EFFECTS OF TOXIC WORKPLACES

*Sybil works in a corporate job and has been in her position for many years. She is a Black woman who has routinely been passed over for promotion. Instead, the company consistently hires less experienced, younger White professionals that she has to train, and who are then positioned to supervise her. To compensate for their lack of knowledge and experience, these supervisors often are disrespectful and hostile. Sybil has become depressed and feels powerless and stressed. She has lost hair and sleep. One of the only ways she has found to relieve her stress is to smoke cigarettes, even though she knows they aren't good for her.*

When you work in toxic places, it affects you holistically. Mentally, you may find yourself having difficulty concentrating. Emotionally, you may find yourself depressed, angry, irritable, anxious, or numb and shut down. Physically, you may find yourself getting sick all the time, suffering from headaches or backaches, nausea, or a compromised immune system. Spiritually, you may feel frustrated if your current position is not aligned with your purpose and gifts. I invite you to consider what this job has cost you: not just time, but energy, health, and well-being.

You may feel stuck due to limited finances, a lack of education, or geographical constraints, but I encourage you to reflect on any level of choice that you do have. Often your despair will increase when you feel stuck and powerless because you believe that no one else will hire you or that you're too old to start over. I invite you to just imagine that there are options even if they are in the same company, but a different department. As long as you surrender to the idea of being stuck, then you will continue showing up in spaces that you have outgrown. This work situation may be all you could have imagined a few months or years ago, but give yourself permission to look again.

When a butterfly emerges, you never see it going back to hang out with the caterpillars because it knows it no longer belongs there. Some of you know in your bones that you have outgrown the position, the company, or the industry that you are in. Some of you are in a cubicle doing busywork that does not fulfill you because you have a vision for entrepreneurship. You may feel stalled, on hold, watching life pass you by. If that is you, homecoming may mean coming out of places that do not reflect, fulfill, or honor you.

## IN THE MEANTIME

For some of you, it is not realistic, practical, or possible to transition at this moment, so you must consider how to stay connected to yourself while you're in a place you don't want to be. It is important to learn how to cope and thrive in restrictive environments. For others, homecoming will mean getting clear that it's time to launch and you are ready to do it. As you come home to yourself, you will gain more clarity about which season you are in—endurance or exit. This may be the season for you to learn how to shift so you are less bothered by the actions of those around you, or this may be the season for you to close that chapter and give yourself a fresh start. Only you can answer the question of which season this is going to be. Coming home to yourself means tapping into your wisdom so you can know the answer for yourself. As you tune in and tell yourself the truth, you will shift from confusion to clarity. As you honor yourself and know yourself, decisions become easier.

For those of you who need to stay where you are for a season, there may be a number of things you can gain from the place you're in. You may learn a new skill, acquire new wisdom, or develop the ability to work with certain people. Decide what you want to gain from your time there, and let that be the center of your focus and motivation. When I was training to be a psychologist, I had to work at multiple rotations or sites. Each assignment was usually for a year. Some of the locations were stressful and disorganized, but I had to stay for the full year. To make that tolerable, I had to look at what the place could offer me. What could I learn there about the job, myself, other people, or life? I invite you to consider what you can gain from the place where you are currently working if you feel you need to stay there. Sometimes what you gain in those valley experiences prepares you for the next chapter of your life. So besides focusing on the next paycheck, look for the treasure in the trash. You may make a lifelong friend there, you may learn negotiation skills or self-advocacy skills that will serve you down the road, or you may learn to disconnect from the drama around you so it does not drain you.

It's a beautiful thing when you can look back over your life and acknowledge the valleys but also see the ways you grew, learned, and cared for yourself along the way. The reality is that most people have work experiences that from the outside look like detours, but actually are important parts of the journey. Let me be clear: you don't have to look for sunshine where there is none. Some experiences are terrible and traumatic, and you can just look back on them and appreciate the fact that you survived and escaped.

## TIME'S UP

*Nathan, a middle-aged Asian American man, could not bear his job another day. He had been disrespected by his supervisors in multiple meetings. He was constantly given impossible work assignments that caused him to work late into the night for no additional pay. He was micromanaged and was in a position with a high turnover rate; yet the managers refused to make any changes to the role. After being there for two years, he developed panic attacks on his way to work and on Sunday nights when he thought about starting a new week. He felt sick to his stomach whenever there were group meetings or his supervisor walked over to his desk. He routinely missed lunch trying to get his work done. He lost trust in his coworkers, as he noticed the environment pitted them against one another. Nathan had graduated at the top of his class and had always done well at other positions. Now his confidence was broken, and he was uncertain if any other employer would hire him. He came home to himself and acknowledged that this job was breaking his spirit, and to survive, he had to get out of there.*

It's important that you tell yourself the truth if your job is creating or exacerbating your depression or anxiety. Be mindful if your dread of going to work reaches the point of emotional distress and possibly physical discomfort. Tune into how you feel when you're on your way to work, while you are there, and when you leave. Pay attention to the messages your body is giving you. Perspiration, knots in your stomach, headaches, a tight jaw, backaches, and tense muscles can all be indicators of a toxic workspace, especially if you have not had those symptoms at other jobs. If you suffer from an anxiety that persists no matter where you are, then you know the job is likely not the issue. If, on the other hand, there are people or circumstances at your job that are causing you intense distress, pay attention to that. If everything associated with your job brings up dread, anxiety, anger, bitterness, and burnout, acknowledge that truth.

One of the challenges with being in that state is that it usually is beyond your ability to mask it. If you hate your job, people often pick up on that, and this can create additional tension in the workplace. If, conversely, you can mask the fact that you hate your job, then you are engaging in a lot of emotional labor, invisible labor that will eventually take a toll on you. Having to be inauthentic for the majority of your day can feel exhausting and can disconnect you further from yourself. The way you build your confidence and connection to yourself is by living from a place of truth.

Tell yourself the truth about what the real issue is in terms of your discontent. Put things in perspective. Do you not like the job, or do you not like one person at the job? Do you dislike office politics, or do you dislike interacting with your coworkers (which would be a problem no matter where you worked)? Try to get a sense of what is truly happening, whether it's poor management, discrimination, or unfair or unsafe work conditions. Give an honest assessment of the things you do and don't like. When you dig deep and see the truth of the issue, it will help you to know what to look out for when you are searching or interviewing at other companies. You don't want to end up going to a different place where the same dynamics are in play.

You want to determine if there is any role you played in the dynamics so you can approach things differently next time. Perhaps you volunteered for too much, and now people expect you to do things that are not in your job description. Perhaps you became too friendly with the supervisor and then became offended when they treated you like everyone else. Perhaps you never asked for a raise, but you noticed that only people who spoke up were given bonuses. Some workplaces are just problematic, and you want to figure out how to navigate those spaces.

*Alona, a Native American woman, was a very hard worker—she took initiative and had wonderful people skills. Her boss noticed her great skills and appreciated her volunteerism. As time went on, her boss gave her more and more tasks but never a promotion or increase in salary. Alona was doing the job of three people. When she tried to remove some of the additional tasks from her plate, her boss was offended and angry. She demanded that Alona continue all the tasks unless she could find someone else to do them. Of course, with no additional pay involved, no one was interested in taking on these responsibilities. Eventually Alona left the job, but when she started a new job, the same thing happened again. To come home to herself, she had to be mindful to not be so quick to try to fill in every gap that she saw. She released her identity as a rescuer, a superwoman, and the glue that held everyone together. She became intentional about focusing on her job only, which wasn't easy because she loved to help others, but she remembered how painful it had been when she spread herself too thin. In her other positions, she'd become physically and emotionally sick and was still barely covering her bills. She told herself the truth and also explored the insecurities that drove her to try to be everything to everyone. She now lives a life of self-compassion without feeling perpetually exploited and overworked.*

Begin to recognize any power you have over the things you do not like about your work life. Also, be honest with yourself about how those things make you feel. Sometimes you might pretend that you're fine when you're not. Your stress might show up in your body, your attitude, or your motivation, and may lead to increased drinking, smoking, sleeping, or even eating.

## SELF-COMPASSION

Give yourself compassion instead of judgment and condemnation. You may blame and shame yourself for how you ended up at this job, but the reality is that when you beat yourself up all the time, the situation and your mental health get worse. Instead, tell yourself the truth about yourself, the job, and your journey here. Then combine self-compassion with the truth: Your job does not define you. Your employer and your coworkers do not define you. If you are not at home within yourself, no job title or promotion is going to fill the internal void. If you make the position the measure of your self-worth and then you get laid off, you are left feeling like you're nothing.

At times we may have looked for outside indicators to tell us who we are, but in this moment of the homecoming journey, let's step away from the lie that people should be treated differently based on their income, education, or title. The truth is that each of us is worthy of care and respect.

Wherever I work, I'm worthy. Even when I don't have a job, I'm still worthy. Homecoming involves peeling away all the things outside of you that you have relied on to validate you, whether that is a title, a relationship, or a certain salary.

## CREATING RITUALS

Wherever you are currently working, I encourage you to create a ritual in the morning before you get to work. Select some ways you can nourish yourself and feed your spirit, so you don't show up empty.

As I mentioned at the beginning of the chapter, I used to work in a very toxic environment. There was always drama, with people crying and cursing in meetings. Working there was emotionally exhausting, and I had to be intentional about taking care of myself before I came to work each day. One morning when I was walking in, my supervisor stopped me on the stairs and said, "Thema, you always look so happy, and I get the feeling it has nothing to do with this place." I told her, "You're right. If I was dependent on this place for my joy, I'd be a miserable person." I told her that I have a spiritual practice that I do every morning, so that I show up to work with my cup already full, instead of needing the job to fill me up.

I invite you to consider developing a practice, a ritual that will feed your spirit before you go to work. For some people, inspirational music is therapeutic; others prefer meditation or prayer. Some people like to start their day reading a sacred text or listening to a podcast. Others start the day with movement—dance, yoga, or a morning walk. Explore to see what feeds you, and then give yourself that gift each day so you are nourished and grounded. The practice doesn't have to end when you leave your house. Be mindful of what you're listening to in the car or on the bus or train to work. Choose a song that puts a smile on your face, affirms your spirit, or makes you want to dance, so by the time you walk into work, you have the confidence, clarity, and calm to sustain you.

You can detox your workspace by filling it with life-giving images, sounds, and scents. You can also spiritually detox your office by arriving early to pray or meditate.

## TEAMWORK MAKES THE DREAM WORK

Next, figure out who your allies and advocates are on the job, those people you connect with, respect, and value. When things are out of order at work, it helps to at least have someone you can catch eyes with, someone who cares about you and can acknowledge the chaos, even if everyone else has adjusted to it. These people can also be a reality check for you because they know the others involved. Sometimes it is challenging to convey the dynamics to someone who has never been in that specific situation. If you have a friend or someone willing to advocate for you at your workplace, it can make a world of difference. That person can also give you helpful suggestions based on their observations and experiences in the same place. You can work together to stabilize, support, and invigorate each other.

## PICK YOUR BATTLES:
## RECLAIM AND PROTECT YOUR PEACE

On the journey home, pick your battles. Often in toxic workplaces, people argue and tear one another down. You will need to be intentional about preserving your energy, recognizing that some things are not worth your time and energy. If something doesn't matter in the grand scheme of things, you don't have to chase it or fight about it. Remember who you are and what your purpose is before you spend a lot of time engaging in something that is being blown out of proportion. As the saying goes, "Don't sweat the small stuff." There will be people who do outrageous things that need to be addressed, but often the things people get worked up about are really small.

Learn not to put your self-esteem, your emotions, and your evaluation of the day in other people's hands. There is an old song by Shirley Caesar that says, "This joy I have the world didn't give to me . . . [and] the world can't take it away." Get to a place where it doesn't steal your joy when co-workers don't invite you to lunch with them or a supervisor calls a lot of unnecessary meetings.

Reclaim yourself so that people cannot easily ruin your day. Decide you will no longer live your life holding your breath, waiting for other people to say you did well. Know in your bones when you did well, even if no one else thanks you, recognizes your contribution, or applauds your efforts. Look at your sacrifice, growth, effort, and results, and know when to affirm yourself with a *Well done*. It is wonderful when you have a supportive supervisor, but if that is not the case, remind yourself about the value of your contributions. As human beings, we appreciate acknowledgment, but if you are working in an environment where that is not going to happen, don't forget to give that recognition to yourself.

## LEAVE WORK AT WORK

*Roland, a thirty-five-year-old Black man, worked in a high-stress, low-reward job. There were perpetual demands and deadlines and a lot of conflict, with people taking out their frustration on one another. His supervisors would humiliate him and pick arguments with him in staff meetings, undermining him in front of people he was supposed to supervise. His manager would ask him about his professional goals and then block him from attaining them. Roland would come home depleted and take out his frustration on his wife. He would swing between talking nonstop about work problems late into the night and refusing to speak to his wife at all. The stress and dissatisfaction of his job took over his life. He looked for escape in food and other women. To save his physical and mental health, as well as his marriage, he had to learn to not internalize the toxicity of his job. Eventually he had to take the huge step of walking away from the job to come home to his authentic self. When he got a new position, he was affirmed and appreciated, but he was left facing the consequences of how he had responded to the toxic workplace.*

As much as possible, leave work at work. Toxic workplaces can consume your life without your even realizing it. Even when you're not there, the job can be at the center of your conversations and your thoughts. Make a decision to protect your time, energy, and yourself by not thinking about that job nonstop. Sometimes you may replay exchanges repeatedly, wondering what you could have said or done differently. This is normal, but you want to be mindful about setting your boundaries so that you cultivate an identity and a life beyond the job.

## CARE, PLEASURE, AND BALANCE

Make a decision to prioritize your care by protecting time for the things that bring you joy. Make the commitment to care for and nourish yourself with healthy food, rest, and time with positive people. You can also nourish yourself with relaxing, enjoyable entertainment. When your day is filled with stress and tension, make a point of cultivating your humor. Laughter is medicine.

Release the stress from your body so you're not holding all the tension of the day in your muscles and in your digestive system. Sexual intimacy can also be a healing space when it is healthy, and can bring release, tenderness, and joy to counter the pressures of your work environment.

Create a life of balance because your work life does not need to be the sum total of your life. Time is valuable, and you spend so many hours of your life working. Become intentional about the way you invest your time outside of work. Choose things, people, and places that fuel you and restore you.

## BE STRATEGIC

When you work in a toxic environment, you need to develop clarity about your strategy and plan for your season there. Identify the decision-makers, the supportive members of your team, and those who consistently create confusion, drama, or negativity. Then begin to think through the various options for making your workplace more tolerable and perhaps even enjoyable. Consider what shifts are needed within you and around you to de-stress or detox your time there. Develop a plan for how to make your time at work more fulfilling, or at the very least, more peaceful. If you're going to stay there, who would you like to improve your relationship with? Who do you need to communicate or collaborate with more, and who do you need to find a way to reduce interaction with? Consider the things that are in your power to do to bring more ease to your day. You can develop both a survival strategy and a thriving strategy in that environment. Being in a toxic workplace without a strategy is a setup for continued emotional stress, fatigue, and perhaps termination.

As you come home to yourself, you can start moving through that place, connected with your inner wisdom. You have gleaned wisdom from what you have observed in that environment and in other contexts with similar personalities, whether at prior jobs or in your family. You are not clueless. Tap into the wisdom within you and within your circle of trusted friends, so you can work there without being consumed by or defined by the toxicity. Your presence, intentions, support team, strategy, and spirit can shift the atmosphere to some degree.

## READY TO LAUNCH

Finally, there are some of you who are ready to launch into a new position at another workplace or to start your own business. Identify what awakens you, what you would do regardless of the money. Look at your skill set, resources, motivation, gifts, and opportunity. If homecoming means you're going to start your own business, then create your business plan and talk to other people who have that kind of business. While some people are withholding, there are others who are willing to share the information that helped them get started. Be open to both donated and paid mentorship, as you want to respect people's time and experience.

As you plan, you move from fantasy to manifestation. Many people are dreamers, but you want to be among those who launch and manifest the vision. To do this, you need to dig into the details. Consider the finances and legal aspects of the business, publicity, promotion, innovation, and distribution. Recognize your strengths and growth areas, and commit to investing in your dream. Being at home with yourself will also mean quality control. You want to create products that are a reflection of you, so be mindful about not cutting corners. You are worthy and capable of excellence. Success will not be easy or instantaneous, but pursuing your purpose is a gift you give yourself.

If you are going to work for someone else, make sure you take time to process and heal from the toxic workplace if possible, so you don't carry bitterness or burnout with you. Start afresh with the wisdom from your past, but not the wounds that can lead to self-sabotage, defensiveness, or isolation.

Whether with someone else's company or your own, prepare for the challenges. Be mindful of the negative experiences from your past and do whatever is in your power to not replicate those dynamics. You don't want to abuse your power the way you saw other people abuse theirs. You don't want to re-create or participate in the negative patterns or cycles you saw at your old position. Give yourself the gift of newness.

As you make the decision to launch and soar, remember that the beautiful thing about flying is that you don't have to be fearless. You just have to be willing to try even if you're afraid. Sometimes we put ourselves on hold because we're afraid that we might fail, but even if you do fail, you can move on from there. Failure does not have to be the end of the road, but a pit along the way. You learn from it and take the knowledge with you for the next launch.

For those who are beginning to look for a new job, cast a wide net. Sometimes we box ourselves in unnecessarily. There might be a new stream, a new position, a new possibility with your name on it. Free yourself from the limitations of the past, whether placed on you by others or by yourself. Get free so you can be at home with your own greatness. Take the blinders off so you can find your next chapter, your next career, your next dimension. When you're at home with yourself, you're committed to being everything you were born to be, nothing less.

## HOMEWORK

If you're at a toxic workplace, tell someone you trust, and share with them what you plan to do about it. This is called having an accountability partner. Sometimes we resign ourselves to misery and lose sight of our power. Whether you are going to work on transforming your attitude or creating change within the institution, share it with your trusted friend. If you're going to start looking for a new job or working on your own business plan, share the commitment with your friend. When we speak things aloud, we take a step toward manifestation. There is power in what you declare and affirm, and that power gets activated when you follow your words with intention and action. See it, speak it, and do it so you can be more at home with yourself even when you're at work.

After every toxic job you have survived, I invite your soul to tell your heart, mind, body, and spirit, "Welcome home."

# CHAPTER TWELVE

# Recovering from Childhood Trauma

Before this chapter begins, let me caution you that sometimes when you read about trauma, it can bring up memories and strong emotions. I encourage you to pace yourself as you read. I do not go into graphic detail about traumatic events, but I describe different types of trauma, the effects, and ways that you can cope. If you find yourself becoming overwhelmed, I encourage you to think about taking a break, taking a cleansing breath, getting a drink of water, listening to some calming music, giving yourself a hug, or reaching out to someone like a friend, therapist, or hotline. Healing is a marathon, not a sprint, so there is no rush to the finish. Take as much time as you need.

*I spent most of my upbringing in Baltimore, Maryland. Baltimore is full of flavor, creativity, and culture. It also has high rates of community violence and poverty. I didn't realize the number of fights I saw growing up was significant until I became a mother. I was amazed when my daughter, who was thirteen at the time, came home stunned because she had seen her first fight ever. I don't remember the first fight I saw, but if I had to guess, I was probably about six or seven years old. Fights were a routine part of the playground and community experience when I was growing up in Baltimore.*

*I moved to Liberia, West Africa, with my parents and brother when I was fourteen. The first year and a half was liberating and wonderful. I was able to see the beauty and brilliance of West Africa, which is often not shown in American media. I embraced and was embraced by the people and the culture. I learned traditional dances at the cultural center and taught ballet and modern at the local dance school. I participated in track and field tournaments and even was crowned Ms. High School Liberia. Unfortunately, toward the end of our second year, a civil war broke out. Fear, violence, and confusion were everywhere. Since we were American, my family and I were able to be evacuated. People I loved were displaced, and some of the people I loved died. When I returned to the United States, I was forever changed, more connected and confident in my roots but also more driven by survivor's guilt from the war.*

You may have wounds from early in life that continue to affect you today. The destruction and discouragement of trauma may have caused you to lose sight of yourself, but the beautiful part about homecoming is the recognition that you are still present. You made it, not without scars or pain, but you made it. The trauma may have caused you to become disconnected, overwhelmed, or even hopeless, but you are present nonetheless.

Your childhood trauma may have involved physical, sexual, psychological, or verbal abuse. You may have experienced neglect or natural disasters, medical trauma or war. It may have occurred in your home, school, or community. Some of you may also have experienced the trauma of oppression, emerging from early encounters with racism, sexism, classism, and every form of oppression that targets you because of your identity, immigration status, or health. Early trauma may have disrupted and derailed you emotionally, sexually, or physically. You may have been the direct target of the trauma, or you may have witnessed it. The trauma may have happened to a loved one in your family or friendship circle. You may have experienced traumatic grief and loss from the incarceration or sudden death of a loved one. No matter the form of trauma, whether it happened in one day or over the course of your childhood, I want you to know that trauma affects you, but it doesn't define you. In other words, there were definite consequences to what you experienced, but those experiences are not the totality of your identity.

The trauma may have been so overwhelming that you felt you had to abandon yourself, disconnect from yourself. It may be hard for you to feel grounded, present, or connected, so give yourself grace and breath. The traumas of childhood can impact you in significant ways, and yet you can still come home to reclaim yourself.

You may even feel, as a result of sexual or physical trauma, that you are disconnected from your body. You may feel that your body betrayed you or made you a target. You may carry shame and fear in your body. This is an opportunity to reclaim all the parts of you, including your body, that were discarded and disrupted. This is an invitation to nourish and care for your whole self. You are worthy of safety, comfort, and affirmation from yourself. Breathe. You may have sought comfort and affirmation in substances, accomplishments, and even unloving partners. Now is the opportunity to give yourself that comfort by coming home to yourself.

You may know that the trauma occurred and that you have not really worked through it, but you may not be aware of the imprint the trauma has had on your life, psyche, relationships, and heart.

## ACKNOWLEDGMENT

*Michelle, an adolescent Latina, was molested by her mother's live-in boyfriend, starting when she was twelve years old. When the molestation escalated two years later from touching to rape, she told her mother. Her mother accused her of lying. The next time her mother had to work late, Michelle knew the abuse would occur again, so she recorded it. She took the recording to school and gave it to her teacher. Michelle's mother was angry with her for getting other people involved in their business. She blamed Michelle for her boyfriend's arrest and continued to call Michelle a liar. Michelle pushed the abuse out of her mind, or at least stopped talking about it. She joined a gang where one of the leaders made her his girlfriend and protected her from the other men in the neighborhood. She was torn because she wanted to go to college and become an architect, but the gang demanded her time, attention, and loyalty. I met Michelle when she was fifteen and ready to come home to a self she couldn't remember. We had to journey back to a time before she experienced failing grades and deferred dreams of college, before the gang initiation, the abuse, and the denial of the abuse. From that place of acknowledgment, she could begin to recover herself and her dreams.*

The first step in healing childhood trauma is to acknowledge that it happened—this in and of itself is huge for many of you. You may have been raised to minimize, deny, bury, and suppress the trauma. People may have ignored it or made you feel that it was insignificant, especially if the perpetrator was a family member or someone the family esteemed in your community. Acknowledgment is not only recognizing that the trauma occurred, but also being aware that it was significant and that you are significant. You may have continued to see the perpetrator and had to pretend it didn't happen or that it didn't matter, but it does. Your safety and well-being matter.

The trauma should not have happened. You may have been pressured to tuck it away or compartmentalize it, but the reality is that trauma often peeks out in various ways. So today, push past family, cultural, and religious pressures to deny, and instead, choose to acknowledge what you experienced. You may have spent years pretending or even convincing yourself that it didn't matter and that you were fine. I invite you to give yourself space not to pretend or perform. The reality is that the smile in your childhood pictures does not tell the full story of those years, so you can push past the expectations, fragility, manipulation, and pressure of others to recognize the truth that your journey has included some pain.

There is a lot of research on adverse childhood experiences (ACEs), and all the evidence points to the long-term consequences of trauma. The severity of the trauma and the number of exposures have an impact on development and well-being holistically, mind and body. The trauma does not end at the moment of the punch, penetration, or abandonment. It sticks with you in numerous ways. You may want to breathe as you reflect on the various assaults, violations, boundary crossings, crimes, and harm that you have experienced and the ways they have affected you.

## EFFECTS OF TRAUMA

*Kevin, a single African American man in his sixties, grew up in the South and was one of the first kids to desegregate an all-White school. On multiple occasions, he had rocks thrown at him by White children and their parents. He was threatened and ostracized. Decades later, he has severe anxiety and a recurring hand tremor. He does not feel comfortable around White people, and his fears are routinely confirmed by the cases of police brutality, racially motivated hate crimes against Black people, and the growing membership of hate groups in the United States. A recent killing of an unarmed Black man and the exoneration of the police officer who took his life have left Kevin tearful, enraged, and tired of being afraid. He specifically sought a Black therapist because he wanted to heal and come home to himself.*

*We had to examine not only the impact of the violations and in-dignities from his adulthood, but also the ways in which he was directly targeted and lacked protection as a child. Kevin has experienced no justice, and as a result, he has no peace.*

As you seek to come home to yourself, be aware of the ways that childhood trauma affected you in the immediate aftermath and the ways it may continue to you affect you now. As you raise your level of awareness, you can better distinguish between your identity and your trauma. When you are not aware of the effects of trauma, you may assume that some of your responses to the trauma are just aspects of your identity or personality; in fact, you can heal and change. You may have experienced depression, suicidal thoughts, rage, irritability, anxiety, confusion, shame, and emotional numbness. You may also have developed post-traumatic stress disorder, which includes avoiding things and people that remind you of the trauma, intrusive thoughts about the trauma, and hypervigilance or guardedness. Others may idealize numbness and praise you for your strength, when actually you are disconnected. Being stoic can help keep you from being overwhelmed when you're in a stressful environment, but when you get to the place where you are shut down or disconnected from any feelings all the time, that is not truly living.

The ways you survived have not always been recognized or celebrated, but they are part of your journey. It may not have been safe for you to feel or to express your feelings in the past. Now in your adulthood, you may find it difficult to acknowledge and express your feelings, or you may be very focused or vigilant about how other people respond to you. Cognitively, or mentally, you may have had difficulty concentrating as a child and even as an adult. You may have struggled in school or had difficulty completing tasks or assignments. This can be a trauma response because the trauma takes so much energy to manage that you are too mentally exhausted to do other things.

You may also have had difficulty taking directions or instructions from people in authority positions, such as teachers or supervisors. You may associate people in power with being abusive, so this can lead you to be combative or defensive whenever you interact with someone who holds power. This can create trouble at school, work, and even home. You may react strongly when it seems someone has authority over you because you are anticipating the worst. This may cause others to label you as aggressive, volatile, oppositional, or a troublemaker, when in reality you are simply afraid of being hurt or taken advantage of. Coming home to yourself will free you from the need to perpetually live in combat mode, preparing for battle.

On the other end of this spectrum is extreme people pleasing. You may find yourself always trying to appease others in the hope that you will be safe if people like you. Without even thinking about it, you may cater to others and neglect your own needs. This is also a survival strategy based on the belief or experience that if others are happy with you, they will not harm you.

You may also look at your life and see that you sabotaged relationships or held people at a distance because of trust issues. You may both long for connection and actively work to block people from really getting to know you. Your relationships may be nonexistent or very superficial because it feels too vulnerable to really let people in. On the other hand, some of you may define yourself by other people's attention and approval, so you may find being alone unbearable. When you constantly need reassurance and validation, people's appreciation is never enough. No matter how much time or attention they give you, you may find yourself constantly questioning if they really care and if you will ever be enough. Pushing people away and constantly seeking others' approval are actually two sides of the same coin, because trauma can lead to doubting yourself and not feeling safe in any space. The sense of emptiness can be so overwhelming that it pulls your attention throughout the day. Consider the ways your early exposure to trauma may continue to affect your relationship choices and approach to intimacy. You may associate relationships with manipulation, games, deception, betrayal, or abandonment. These beliefs may keep you disconnected from yourself and others.

Consider relationship patterns that you may want to heal as you come home to yourself:

- Do you constantly put your partner through tests?
- Do you routinely withhold information from your partner?
- Does love feel scary?
- Do you fear that you are not enough for your partner?
- Do you make it a rule to not share your true feelings?
- Do you approach sex as a conquest or a performance?
- Do you need to be intoxicated or high to have sexual intimacy?
- Do you shut down during sex, waiting for it to be over?
- Do friends, family members, and/or romantic partners call you controlling?

Trauma can also result in your neglecting yourself. You may neglect your hygiene, medical appointments, rest, or even food. The trauma response can also show up as hoarding or neglecting the space around you in other ways.

Childhood trauma can affect your religious or spiritual beliefs as well. Abusive authority figures can translate into your view of God. If you view God as angry, unloving, and punitive, this may stem from your trauma history or from exposure to someone with unresolved trauma. You may feel rejected and filled with shame and guilt, which permeates your faith experience. On the other hand, some of you may have found that your faith saved you. You may not trust people, but hold on to the idea that God is your only friend and confidant. Both ends of the spectrum can emerge from traumatic events. Spiritual or religious teachings that leave you feeling unloved and trapped are traumatizing and can keep you from your homecoming.

# RECOVERY:
# IS IT OVER?

*Khadija was physically and verbally abused by her parents throughout her childhood. Sometimes a favorite aunt would try to protect her, but this was usually not successful and would sometimes make things worse. Her parents left bruises on her body and her mind. Based on her culture and religion, she is not supposed to move out of the house until she marries. Even though she is an adult, she still lives at home with her parents, who often berate her by calling her lazy, stupid, and ugly. They treat her like a burden, put her down for being single, and occasionally slap her. Khadija wants to heal and come home to herself, but she is still living with and dependent on her parents, whose words and deeds have led to Khadija's depression, suicidal thoughts, and insomnia. She does not have the safety to fully come home to her authentic self.*

It is very hard to heal if your safety is still compromised. If you are living with abusive parents as an adult, or if you are currently with an abusive partner, you are in survival mode. You can work on coping and surviving, but healing and freedom can come only when you are in a place of psychological and physical safety. If you are still in danger, you need to maintain a constant level of vigilance to survive. I invite you to consider whether you are currently on a battlefield or whether you can work on taking off some of your armor. I invite you to consider whether you are in a safe enough place to breathe and tell the truth. How risky is it for you to come home to yourself in this season of your life? And if it is not safe, is there anything you can do to improve your safety? You may be facing high-risk challenges, such as a partner who has threatened to take your children or to report you to immigration, or who keeps a loaded weapon. If these or other factors are currently preventing your escape, I encourage you to get help from resources in your area to address the dangers you are facing. Give yourself compassion as you try to obtain glimpses of home within yourself, even if you cannot live from that place throughout your day.

If you have experienced the trauma of oppression, I know that oppression is ongoing, so there is always the possibility of discrimination, hatred, and stigma. I encourage you to be intentional about continuing to affirm home within yourself and with your community and trusted allies. Also, continue on to the next chapter, where I will discuss oppression more in depth.

## SELF-CARE

Once you acknowledge the trauma and its impact on your life, commit to giving yourself care and nourishment. As you become intentional about being gentle and loving toward yourself, you begin to heal the wounds of those experiences that dishonored you. As you begin to show yourself love, you resist and reject the false beliefs of your unworthiness. Intentionally begin taking steps to interrupt the cycle of self-neglect, and instead make choices to protect and preserve your wellness. You do not have to continue re-creating the painful patterns of the past. You can shift the story of your family and your community. You do not have to treat yourself in the same way as those who mistreated you. Your lowest seasons, however long they were, do not have to be your final destination. As an adult, you can begin to live for your highest good by choosing safety and self-care when it is in your power to do so. You reject the imprint of the trauma when you are caring and loving toward yourself. Your self-compassion paves the road back home to yourself.

## RELEASING SHAME

Part of your healing journey involves releasing the shame that often accompanies trauma. Shame causes you to feel like something is wrong with you, instead of focusing on the fact that something wrong was done *to* you. The violations you experienced are the responsibility of the offender, the perpetrator, the one who mistreated you. They are accountable for their actions. You are not responsible for the ways you were hurt or left unprotected as a child. Shame may have been placed on you as a child, and you may have carried that shame in your body, heart, mind, and spirit. You may have felt ashamed of who you are and lived from that place of shame, which can set you up for further violation and victimization. Shed the shame so you can move away from being embarrassed or even disgusted with yourself. As you come home, awaken to the truth that the shame you have been carrying does not belong to you. It is based on lies and misperceptions of your identity and the past.

To journey home, begin to work through and reject the shame and the self-blame of violations in childhood and even adulthood. Bring to your awareness any childhood experiences that you have been holding yourself responsible for. Bring to your awareness anything you've been blaming yourself for that is not your baggage to carry. Raise your consciousness about the things that you have been through that were not your fault. You should not have needed the knowledge and skills of an adult in your childhood and adolescence. It may be difficult to stop blaming yourself for things you've been carrying for years, but I encourage you to envision yourself at the age when you experienced the trauma. Can you stop putting the expectations of adulthood on your seven-, twelve-, even seventeen-year-old self? You can make a decision to not be angry with the younger version of yourself, who did the best they could at the time. I invite you to look back at yourself with grace and compassion. Look back and see the child you were, not the adult you are now. Make a decision to take the bricks of blame, condemnation, and judgment off your back. Take away the punishment and welcome yourself back home.

## HEALING TRUST

While a part of your healing is internal, another part involves trusting yourself and others enough to break out of isolation and make connection. Relationships rooted in respect and compassion are healing. They can be therapeutic and help you reprogram your ideas about yourself and others. When you allow yourself to be seen authentically by others, you move closer to your homecoming. Being at home with yourself is powerful, but being home in the presence of another is liberating. Trauma teaches you to be suspicious, cautious, and vigilant. It teaches you to trust no one. To come home to yourself and to heal, you must reject that script and begin to risk being honest and present with others. In this season, you can let yourself leave the island of hyperindependence and allow yourself the gift of connection and transparency. Survivors learn to mask their thoughts and feelings, but as you come home to yourself, you learn to take the mask and costume off. You learn to come off the stage and trust the possibility of relationship, interconnection, and intimacy.

The risk of trusting others also involves the risk of trusting yourself. Sometimes you lose trust in yourself because you have experienced difficulties that you were not able to prevent. Healing and restoration from those childhood wounds requires beginning to trust yourself and knowing that self-trust does not require perfectionism. You may not see every danger coming, and you might not get everything right, but at your core, you can begin to trust yourself more. Trust yourself to work through the difficulties, to grow, to unfold, to manifest, and to have goodness within you. As you start to shatter the shame of the childhood trauma and emerge as an adult worthy of love and goodness, you begin to trust yourself to navigate life's journey. None of us is perfect, but with patience and support, trust yourself to figure out your next step, and then the step after that, and so on. So take a breath. Trust that as you keep moving forward, the landscape within you can shift from midnight to daybreak. Outlast midnight. Each day will not be perfect, but trust the spirit within you to outlast the traumatic echoes of the past and even the challenges of the present.

## REFLECTION ON SURVIVING AND THRIVING

*I am a sexual assault survivor. After coming home to myself, I became a volunteer for the local rape crisis center so I could be an advocate, crisis counselor, and prevention educator. Before the age of twenty, I was going into elementary schools to teach children about "good touch and bad touch," as well as where and how they could get help if anyone was hurting them. I went to graduate school to study clinical psychology with an emphasis on trauma recovery. It has been meaningful for me to walk with others on the healing journey back home to themselves, and I am grateful for those who helped me on the journey home to myself. In the process, I recovered my voice, my heart, my spirit, my thoughts, and my body.*

I'm so glad you made it through your childhood, that you survived physically, and now it is my desire that you would survive emotionally and spiritually. I invite you to envision yourself as not just surviving, but as thriving and manifesting. In fact, there is much more to life than living in survival or warrior mode. I invite you to consider post-traumatic growth. As you grow in your awareness of yourself, deepen your relationships, and learn to appreciate your new season and spiritual wellness, you will continue to come home to the miracle of who you are.

## HOMEWORK

Another approach to emotional healing in trauma recovery is the expressive arts. If it feels right to you, consider creating a piece of art that reflects your intention to release shame and self-blame for childhood wounds. You may want to write a poem or a song, choreograph a dance, paint a picture or make a collage, or you may want to write a love letter to your younger self. For your self-care, center the art on the healing journey, not on reenacting the actual events of the trauma. If engaging in art does not align with you, you may want to research someone who is a survivor of childhood trauma and read about what may have helped them to survive.

I invite your soul to tell the childhood and adulthood versions of your heart, mind, body, and spirit, "Welcome home."

# CHAPTER THIRTEEN

# Resisting Oppression

When I was a child in the 1970s, a fancy new hotel opened in downtown Baltimore, where I lived. As a special treat, my dad took our family there to eat. We got dressed up and were so excited to see the beautiful hotel. We were the only Black family there. We sat there as everyone around us was served, including people who arrived long after us. I watched my father, who had participated in sit-ins and protests, including the March on Washington, as his eyes went from relaxed joy to anger. Eventually he had to go and speak with the manager to demand that we be served. We ate in awkward silence and left with the weight of racism hanging over us.

Years later, in my senior year of high school, I had to go meet with my guidance counselor. I was an A student in honors classes, and my parents had always prepared me and my brother for college. When I enthusiastically showed my White guidance counselor the list of schools I wanted to apply to, she looked skeptical, offered no words of encouragement, but instead suggested that I apply to safer, more realistic schools. When I was accepted into Duke University and Stanford University, among other schools, *she was silent. A White student who had been accepted into a lower-ranked school was given a tribute on the school loudspeaker, while we were all told to celebrate and to be proud of and inspired by this student. A generation earlier, my mother had had a similar experience with her White guidance counselor attempting to talk her out of college and instead encouraging her to apply to secretarial school. A generation before that, my grandmother had moved from North Carolina to New York to pursue a nursing training program. She was turned away from the program because Blacks were not allowed. She found work as a housekeeper before going to work at an orphanage. There has been a history of anti-Black racism that has taken the form of overt hate crimes, legalized oppression, institutionalized discrimination, and covert messages that are meant to reduce and invalidate our worth and possibility.*

While much of our reflection on homecoming has centered on the psychological aspects of the journey, I want to acknowledge those of us who not only have experienced a lack of grounding within ourselves, but have also experienced cultural and political homelessness, a sense of being disconnected, rejected, and marginalized culturally and politically. Immigrants have spoken about this experience of not feeling fully home anywhere. People who have been discriminated against because of racism and sexism also search for this sense of community and belonging, while spending large portions of their days in spaces that are not welcoming. People who have been marginalized for multiple reasons have been silenced even within political movements meant to empower members of their community. For example, disabled, trans, and BIPOC women have written about discrimination within the women's movement. Similarly, movements that focus on racial justice have often been silent about the discrimination facing women and sexual minorities in oppressed racial groups. In this chapter, I invite you to reflect on your various identities and the ways marginalization and oppression have affected your journey home to yourself. For some of you, homelessness has been more than a metaphor. Housing insecurity may have been or currently is a part of your lived daily reality. In fact, physical homelessness is directly related to political homelessness, as our political realities shape our access to care and resources.

In Western psychology, many therapists argue that the only thing that matters is what *you*, the individual, thinks, feels, and does. According to these psychologists, you can't change anything outside of yourself, so you have to focus on you. There are challenges and limitations to this approach because it ignores the reality that each of us has been raised and lives in a context in which there are multiple hierarchies of power. Some people are targeted for harm, marginalized, and institutionally and systematically left out and discarded. When the therapist takes those things into consideration, the lives of the marginalized make sense. It is not surprising that you lost track of yourself, discounted yourself, or doubted yourself. Your emotional and behavioral responses make sense when the therapist does not ignore the realities of your lived experience. Just as it would not make sense to work with a rape survivor and ignore the rape, it is also deeply problematic to work with someone who has been stigmatized and discriminated against and ignore those experiences.

I invite you to consider your experiences with oppression, discrimination, and stigma. It is important to your homecoming journey that you address the wounds of oppression and internalized oppression. Internalized oppression is when you come to believe the lies you've been told about yourself. I invite you to reflect on the lies that you have been told, directly or indirectly, about the groups you belong to. There are stereotypes and lies about Black people, Latinos, Asians, Native Americans, and Middle Easterners. Lies are perpetuated about people living with mental illness, neurodiversity, and physical disabilities. There are widely accepted untruths about body size, income, education, and country of origin. There are false ideas that are routinely and systematically circulated about people based on their gender, sexuality, and religious affiliation. There are even stereo-types that are widely accepted about people based on their age. These messages carry weight. They translate into how people are treated, oppor-tunities they are afforded or denied, and even the health care they receive. Consider the negative assumptions you make about the marginalized groups you are a part of. Oppression teaches you to despise, fear, or to be ashamed of your community. Oppression is thick, pervasive in society, and we are bombarded with these messages from childhood. Consider the bill-boards you drive past daily, the advertisements and the shows you watch, and the magazines you read. Consider who is present and who is absent, and for those who are present, what messages are being promoted?

You have been given messages about who is beautiful and who is smart, who is likely a criminal and who is likely a trusted leader. Stereotypes and stigma are not random. They grant and protect power. These lies influence how others see us and respond to us, and they can also affect how we see ourselves and other members of our community.

In social psychology, there's a construct called the halo effect, which is when a positive association about someone in one area leads to positive associations about that person in other areas. We can think about the im-plications for children from racial groups whose beauty is often denied and for children who are less well groomed for a number of reasons. If teachers believe a child is attractive and well groomed, they are more likely to as-sume the child is also smarter, kinder, and friendlier and a better student than peers who are deemed plain, unattractive, or disheveled. The reality is that oppression is present in our world and can have an impact on every-thing from the prenatal care your mother received to your present-day physical, mental, and financial well-being.

If you are a member of a marginalized group, you might have come to feel less valuable, or you might feel the stress of knowing that others have deemed you less valuable. Your dreams might have been diluted or deferred due in part to discrimination, and your self-image and self-esteem might have been negatively affected by it. You might have been given the message that you have to try twice as hard to compete against those who are privileged, or you might have been made to feel hopeless or powerless to counter the forces working against you.

I want to tell you that the beliefs you have internalized about your self-worth did not originate in your head. You have been fed racist messages about standards of beauty since the day you were born. Not only do the messages come from advertisements by large corporations, but they can also be internalized and passed down by family members. Consider who among your siblings or cousins was considered attractive. Which features were celebrated, and which were rejected? Did you hear messages growing up about good hair or bad hair? Was straight textured hair celebrated over tightly curled hair? Were blue eyes celebrated over brown eyes? Your family may have bought into colorism, the idea that someone with a lighter complexion is more attractive than someone with a darker complexion. Growing up, I was aware of this in the African American community, but as an adult I came to learn that colorism exists in Asian and Latino communities as well and that there is a global skin-bleaching industry that is particularly pervasive in Africa and Asia. Facial features and body shape have also been ridiculed or idealized along racist and sexist lines. Consider the expectations that were put on your shoulders as a child to live up to standards of beauty, femininity, or masculinity that are the opposite of who you are.

## CONSCIOUSNESS RAISING

*Sekou is a West African immigrant who comes from a family of successful entrepreneurs. When he got his first job in the United States, it was his first time working for someone outside of his family. He was shocked and overwhelmed by the overt racism and discrimination he experienced directly and witnessed toward other Black people at the company. He was baffled at how pervasive it was and how no one seemed to be willing to address it. Sekou sought out the African Americans at the job, but he felt embarrassed at their response. They were astonished that he was shocked and told him to get used to the mistreatment, as there was nothing they could do about it. He came to me for therapy to understand what was happening to him, how it was affecting him, and what he could do about it. Sekou, who had been confi-dent and self-assured throughout his life, now found himself pow-erless, confused, and in need of justice and safety to find his way home.*

Liberation psychology, or decolonizing psychology, calls for us to pay attention to the impact of oppression on our lives. To come home to yourself, you must recognize that the issues you have with your identity, health, and wellness are not solely a product of your individual effort. You exist in systems of oppression, and simply being positive and hardworking does not erase that reality.

Your liberation is not solely about shifting your attitude but also requires us to collectively work to increase equity, safety, and justice in our society. When you become aware of the realities of stereotypes and discrimination, a lot of formerly puzzling things will make sense, and with clarity comes empowerment to better navigate the world while taking care of your wellness. At the same time, you may also feel some level of depression, anxiety, or anger about the injustices that you and others have had to face.

The fact that girls are more likely to have body image issues is not a coincidence or the fault of each individual girl. Girls are being raised in a society that devalues them. When Black and Latino children feel insecure or have impostor syndrome, this is not a product of their own dysfunctional thinking. They are coming of age in educational institutions that often don't celebrate people who look like them among esteemed thinkers, inventors, and leaders. Black and Latino representatives are either absent from the curriculum or presented in negative or powerless ways. An LGBTQ+ young adult who has been harassed by peers and rejected by family and now has suicidal thoughts cannot be helped by a therapist who believes the problem is rooted in negative thought patterns. We exist in context. Your environment affects and shapes you. To come home to yourself, you will need to see the systems and messages that have influenced you.

A famous proverb teaches, "As a (wo)man thinks, so is (s)he." Oppression programs our thinking and the thinking of others. That oppression has to be actively challenged, unlearned, and dismantled so we can all come home to ourselves. Oppression intentionally seeks to control thought to restrict action and protect the status quo and imbalance in power.

Many of us are psychologically in bondage with invisible chains. When discrimination is present, but we tell people that if they just try hard enough, everything will work out for them, we deny the existence of those chains and discredit the person's efforts. I invite you to consider any ways that you were taught to devalue yourself and to want to be different from who you actually are. If you have been stigmatized, you were taught to betray, erase, and even reject yourself. You may have been taught to alter your speech, your hair, your style, and even your feelings to be more acceptable to others.

I invite you to consider who benefits from your insecurities, your sense of inadequacy, and your deflated dreams. There are beneficiaries to oppression, whether they acknowledge it or not; and we are all members of multiple groups, so we may be targets of oppression because of some aspects of our identities, as well as beneficiaries of other people's oppression because of different aspects of our identities. To come home to yourself is to acknowledge and own both the ways you have been targeted and the ways that you have been privileged. When I can see the fullness of the picture with honesty, I am ready to come more fully home to the truth of my life's journey. I have been targeted based on my identity as a woman and as a Black person and the intersection of the two identities, which shows up as gendered racism. Kimberlé Crenshaw developed the construct of intersectionality, which highlights the experience of being a member of multiple oppressed groups.

I have privilege related to being able-bodied, heterosexual, cisgender, and Christian in the United States (although there are other countries in which Christians are persecuted). The ways you are targeted can disconnect you from yourself, and the ways you are privileged can disconnect you, too. When you are targeted by oppression, you may develop insecurity, impostor syndrome, and even shame about your identity. You may also develop double consciousness and vigilance, where you need to always consider how persons outside of your community may view or judge you, instead of feeling free to be your authentic self. If you are a part of the privileged group, along with disconnecting from compassion and empathy for others, you may disconnect from yourself by viewing yourself as the "norm" without ever seeing yourself as a full human being. For example, people who are White are less likely to have given thought to their Whiteness or to their specific ethnicity, such as Italian or French heritage. When you see your identity more fully, you can disrupt and dismantle the barriers that keep you from yourself.

Multicultural feminist therapy, womanist therapy, liberation therapy, and Black psychology, among other approaches, are based on an appreciation of the impact of cultural oppression and the role of justice and cultural connection as pathways to healing and wellness.

## DECOLONIZE PSYCHOLOGY

*Camila is a middle-aged Latina adult who grew up as one of only a few Latinas in her private school. She experienced discrimination from teachers and students, as well as nonstop racist "jokes" about Latinos and sexual harassment and objectification from boys in the school. She had been to counseling before to address her anxiety and grief related to illness and death in her family, but she had never discussed with her former therapists her experiences with oppression, discrimination, and harassment as a youth and an adult. The more she discussed it, the more instances she remembered, and she realized how much unresolved grief and pain she was carrying. She needed a safe space to see the wounds, so she could come home to herself.*

Colonial psychology assumes that Western psychology is the only path to healing; it also engages in gaslighting or victim-blaming of oppressed groups by assuming that their thinking is the problem, without acknowledging societal contributors to their difficulties. To decolonize psychology is to acknowledge Indigenous ways of healing and the needs to disrupt the trauma and stress of oppression.

To decolonize your mind is to reject the lies you have been told about your unworthiness and to take the radical step of claiming and reclaiming your identity as an inheritance, a gift, and a treasure. To be a marginalized person and still know that you are beautiful, intelligent, and significant is revolutionary. Come home to yourself and reject the narrow-mindedness foundational to oppression. Those who suffer from such tunnel vision work overtime to talk you out of your power, trying to convince you that your features, your hair, your size, your skin, your sexuality, your gender, your race, your migration status, and your spirituality make you unacceptable. You are not disqualified from living a full life. You deserve safety, dignity, and respect. As you decolonize your mind, you recognize that the ways you and your community have been treated are not reflective of your worth.

## MICROAGGRESSIONS

*Naomi is a successful Jewish woman who is admired by many but still experiences great insecurity and shame. We had discussed marginalization that she'd personally experienced before she revealed that her mother had physical and psychological disabilities. Naomi had never named and processed the impact it had on her as a child to see people regularly stare at, reject, and mistreat her mother. She felt guilt for the times she had been ashamed of her. Her mother had never experienced an overt hate crime, but the daily invalidations and slights against her had a painful impact. Ableism affects not just the person with the disability but also their loved ones.*

Among the violations that oppressed groups experience are microaggressions, which are daily indignities directed at them because of their marginalized identities. These insults, invalidations, slights, and put-downs are directed toward people of color, women, LGBTQ+ persons, disabled persons, religious minorities, and immigrants, among others. These experiences are subtle, so they are often overlooked, but they have a cumulative effect over time. The person responsible for the microaggression may be unaware of their actions, but the impact is still harmful.

Psychological and spiritual labor are required to hold on to your value in a world where microaggressions are pervasive. Oppression in its various manifestations serves to keep you distracted and disconnected. Combating oppression requires being at home within yourself and joining others to address oppressive forces, systems, and practices. Refuse to erase or dilute yourself to gain the approval of people in power. Refuse to distance yourself from your community. Anything and anyone that requires you to lose you is not worth it.

## HEALING THE STRESS AND WOUNDS OF OPPRESSION

*Paulette, a forty-four-year-old mother, moved into a beautiful gated community. She was the only Black woman in the complex.*

*One day she was walking from her car into the clubhouse. A White woman who lived in the complex blocked Paulette's path and asked if she was visiting someone. Paulette refused to answer, knowing that if she had been White, the woman would not have questioned her presence. The woman declared that the clubhouse was only for residents. Paulette tried to walk around the woman, but she physically blocked Paulette and started screaming that she needed to explain what her business was on the premises or leave immediately. Paulette began trembling with outrage, and the woman told her that if she didn't leave, she would call the police. Paulette screamed that the woman couldn't stop her from going into her own clubhouse. The woman called the police and began crying as she told the operator that she felt unsafe because a Black woman had broken into the community and was threatening her. When the police arrived, someone from the clubhouse finally came outside to see what was happening. They confirmed that Paulette lived in the community. Paulette got back in her car, drove to her house, and called me from her driveway, sobbing. She was sitting in front of her dream house, living the nightmare of racism. She had a new house, but not a home.*

Once you have raised your consciousness and acknowledged oppression and its impact on your life, find safe spaces to name and share your experiences. As you shatter the silence, you affirm your dignity and humanity. You might find safe spaces within your family or community, with friends and loved ones, in therapy or with faith leaders, or even in spaces that you create and cultivate. A part of coming home to yourself includes rejecting internalized oppression, so learning more about your identity and affirming it will help to reverse the lies of oppression. Any therapy that ignores the impact of oppression on your life is incomplete and does not empower you to counter internalized oppression. Learning about your community and culture is medicine.

Giving yourself space to feel your grief and anger, as well as any other emotions, is an important part of your healing journey. It is also important to choose healthy over unhealthy coping strategies as much as possible. The stress and strain of oppression can be overwhelming, and unhealthy coping strategies such as emotional eating, substance dependence, retail therapy (excessive shopping to alleviate distress), self-harming behaviors (such as cutting), taking out frustration on family and friends, or isolating yourself can create more difficulties and distress. Instead, choose coping strategies that affirm and support you, such as journaling, talking to people you trust, expressive arts, spiritual practices, self-care, physical activity, and connecting with nature (gardening, hiking, etc.).

## RESIST

Western psychology usually addresses trauma solely by helping individuals shift their thinking and choose behaviors that are calming and that increase their ability to tolerate distress. These methods alone do not encourage the client to actively engage in anti-oppression efforts. Resistance is a key aspect of healing that is not in Western models of trauma recovery. In liberation, womanist, Black, and social-justice-oriented psychology, resisting oppression is considered an integral part of healing and wellness for marginalized community members.

Traditional Western psychology is built on the idea that the problem, and therefore the solution, lies within you. Decolonized and liberation psychology recognize that oppression is at the root of a lot of our distress and must be addressed in order for us to truly feel at home. While decolonizing focuses on removing the barriers put in place by colonization and oppression, liberation centers the growth, wholeness, and wellness of individuals and communities.

Resistance takes many forms. There is the internal resistance of rejecting the lies of oppression and affirming your worth and value. Resistance can mean engaging in rest, joy, and love, which radically rejects the idea that marginalized people do not have the right to joy and must perpetually labor to prove their worth. There is also the resistance of activism and advocacy, which can take the form of participating in protests, circulating petitions, running for office, creating new policies, boycotting discriminatory companies, and even engaging in artivism, which is using your creativity to raise awareness and counter oppression.

Resist retreating and disconnecting from yourself. Resist accepting negative treatment that should be unacceptable. Resistance goes beyond coping. Coping helps you manage distress in the moment, but it is not a long-term solution. Resistance shifts you and society so that oppression does not have the final say in your life. For marginalized people, loving yourself is an active fight because you are bombarded with messages that try to convince you to be ashamed of yourself and to believe that you are less than because of your identity, when the truth is that you are more than enough.

When you are at home within yourself, you can both love yourself and actively engage in creating a society that has to see, acknowledge, and respond to you with justice. It is a revolutionary, radical act of resistance to embrace yourself in a society that screams that you are unacceptable as you are. Declare your worthiness, and with each declaration, come home to yourself.

You are worthy. You are altogether lovely. You are beautiful inside and out. You carry wisdom, creativity, and gifts. Lean into the truth of who you are, instead of buying into the power structure that teaches you to strain and stress to be something you don't have to be. When you recognize your worth, you will also be free enough to celebrate the beauty, wisdom, and greatness of others without anger, envy, or insecurity. Oppression teaches us that only a few can be special or worthy. Reject that mindset; there is enough room for each of us.

Justice work is mental health work. When you have the courage to name and address oppression, you heal and liberate yourself and others. As you come home to yourself, you also see the ways in which various forms of oppression are interconnected, so you do not need to limit yourself to fighting only the oppression that affects you. Instead, stand in opposition to all forms of oppression. As you create spaces where everyone can show up in the fullness of who they are safely and abundantly, you activate homecoming in those around you.

People at home within themselves will not sit back in silence and powerlessness while others are oppressed based on their sexuality, race/ethnicity, gender, disability, income, migration status, age, religion, nationality, or size. Homecoming births agency, action, activism, and world changers. This is the secret of homecoming. There is so much untapped power and potential within you, yet the reality of oppression often leaves you too distracted and discouraged to tap into it. As you come home to yourself, you are liberated to be everything you were born to be, nothing less.

Either you actively resist the oppressive status quo or your silence allows it to continue unchecked. When you name and disrupt oppression with your mindset, words, and actions, you dismantle it.

Consider who you would be if you had grown up knowing your worth, without the shackles of oppression. Imagine if your intelligence, talent, abilities, and beauty were not questioned or degraded based on stereotypes and stigma. Imagine what you could have done with all the energy that was required to counter being underestimated, bullied, harassed, silenced, rejected, invalidated, and oppressed. All of that took a lot out of you, and yet you have come so far. You need to really take that in and appreciate yourself. You may have judged yourself harshly, comparing yourself to people who did not have to carry the same weights on their backs. Give yourself credit for being where you are, given the uphill journey and the efforts designed to block you.

# COMMUNITY

*Louis is a gay Catholic Latino man who grew up in a tight-knit, loving family and community. The love and support shifted when he came out. His mother was heartbroken, and his father was angry and embarrassed. Louis was rejected by his family and church—people he thought would always be there for him. For a while, Louis thought embracing his sexuality meant he had to surrender his faith. When he moved to a new area that had a larger LGBTQ+ community, he discovered inclusive churches where he was accepted and loved. Louis felt affirmed by God and free to affirm himself. He was spiritually and emotionally at home and hoped one day to be able to reconnect with his family as well. One of his sisters stays in touch with him and gives him hope that reconciliation is possible.*

My hope for you on this homecoming journey is that you create and cultivate a beloved community, a space in which there is mutual love, respect, and appreciation. Create spaces of ease, where you have nothing to prove and freedom to gain. Create spaces that are not built on shame and self-blame, but full of intentional mutual care. These spaces will affirm you and remind you that you matter. You need space where you can breathe and be yourself. You need space where people do not deny or minimize or oppress. You deserve space where you are seen and appreciated in the fullness of who you are, and where you do not have to leave any part of yourself at the door. You deserve a community where your humanity is not up for debate and requires no justification or defense.

## HOMEWORK

--------------------------------------------------------------------

Research someone who has a similar background to your own, whose life's work you appreciate and who is a source of inspiration. They may share your race, nationality, gender, sexuality, religion, disability, migration status, or age. Read about the person or watch a video about their life. Consider the lessons you want to learn from their life, and then tell someone else about this person. Oppression misleads and misinforms, leaving many to believe only straight, cisgender, White, able-bodied men are praiseworthy. Celebrate people like yourself as you come home.

After all you have survived, and after all your ancestors survived, I invite your soul to tell your heart, mind, body, and spirit, "Welcome home."

# Welcome Home: The Journey Continues

W elcome Home!
It has been my honor to journey with you through these pages and stages. I hope you were able to:

1. Recognize your signs of disconnection.
2. Increase your capacity and skills to reconnect with yourself.
3. Navigate the roadblocks on your journey.

It is my heart's desire that you are closer to yourself, more at home psychologically and spiritually. Homecoming is an ongoing process. I hope you will continue this process with journaling, art, spiritual practice, *The Homecoming Podcast*, and perhaps therapy.

## RELAPSE PREVENTION: REJECTING THE PULL OF DISCONNECTION

Sometimes when you complete a book, a retreat, or a series of therapy sessions, you may feel that you are finished working on yourself. This can be followed by disappointment when new challenges or even old problems arise. You may question if you made any progress at all. Coming home to yourself doesn't mean there won't be any more difficult days or seasons, but it does mean that you are better equipped to honor yourself and not abandon yourself on the journey. With greater self-awareness, you can more quickly tune into the moments, circumstances, or relationships that pull you away from your authentic self, and then correct your course. At the end of each day or week, I encourage you to check in with yourself and consider how you remained connected to the truth of who you are, as well as what made you lose sight of yourself. By engaging in these regular check-ins, you increase the likelihood that being at home within yourself will become a way of life, instead of an occasional event. When you do notice that you are becoming disconnected, revisit the strategies in this book and recognize the roadblocks for what they are: obstacles along the way but not your final destination.

## COJOURNERS:
## COMMUNITY FOR THE JOURNEY

I intentionally shared parts of my story with you because I want you to know you are not in it alone. I also shared stories of other people's lives (with their identities protected) so you would know there are many people from all walks of life who are moving toward their own homecoming. If this book was a blessing to you, gifting a copy to a friend may provide you with someone to talk with in more detail about your journey. Authenticity and self-acceptance are contagious. If you are surrounded by people who pressure you to conform and self-censor, homecoming becomes more difficult to maintain. I hope you seek out or nurture relationships with people who celebrate and honor your commitment to coming home to yourself. Having a friend, partner, or community that affirms the importance of authenticity and liberation can empower you to hold on to your awakenings and breakthroughs.

## CONTINUED GROWTH

While I shared strategies for moving past a number of roadblocks on the journey home, I want you to know that the goal is not ultimately to return to who you were before encountering the roadblocks, but to actually grow in the aftermath of those detours and challenges. Although life events can derail and disconnect you, I invite you to be mindful of the very real possibility of growth, thriving, and flourishing. Your identity may have been diluted and censored your entire life, so I invite you to consider what it means for you to shine and soar in the fullness of who you are, even if you have never experienced that before. An important thing to understand about post-traumatic growth is that it can coexist with distress. In other words, you can still take note of your growth, even while you may continue to struggle with your sleep or your confidence. Try not to let the challenges block your view of progress.

Sometimes we mistakenly give credit to our trauma and stress for our growth. But there are people who have experienced the same sources of stress and trauma who did not grow as a result of it. Be mindful of your language. It is not the rape, war, child abuse, or racism that made you a better, wiser, or stronger person. It is the ways in which you were able to manage, cope with, and heal those experiences, with the help of internal and external resources that empowered your growth. If you are not careful, you will overlook the role of your thought processes, cultural resources, spiritual practices, artistry, therapy, and social support in rebuilding your life.

You are a living, breathing miracle. Given what you have survived, many would not predict that you would be where you are today, and yet here you are. You are remarkable. The ways you survived may not have always looked perfect, but you fought to reclaim yourself, and that is worthy of celebration. There are some people, systems, institutions, and barriers that may have slowed down your journey or put some detours in your path, and yet you have the voice, the agency, and the capacity to manifest your authentic self.

Despite oppression, medical conditions, and financial realities, you have been able to navigate the world and bring some dreams into reality.

I celebrate the ways in which you have taken ownership of your psychological and spiritual development and extended gentleness, self-compassion, and grace to yourself. As you grow, you move away from self-sabotage and shame and toward self-acceptance and self-love, so that you do not cooperate with individuals or systems that have sought to destroy or break you. Refuse to agree with anything that is harmful to your wellness. I'm excited about how you are choosing to pull the wisdom out of your wounds to inform your path forward as you continue to learn and discover new facets of yourself. As you grow and change, embrace these new developments with wonder.

You might have grown in strength amidst tears or setbacks, and you have made beautiful steps in the journey home. Your growth may also show up in a new gentleness, compassion, and tenderness toward yourself and others. You may have realized you can lower the wall around your heart and actually feel. You have had the presence of mind to engage in the radical act of slowing down and tending to yourself. You have engaged in the revolutionary act of caring for others. Despite every societal message that tells you to shut down, isolate, and hoard, you show up with a generosity of spirit, and that is a sacred gift of your homecoming. Breathe and embrace it. Breathe and embrace you. Thank you for sticking with the journey and seeing it through. You are worthy of being at home within yourself.

### Closing Blessing

*May you find* ease *within yourself.*
*May your* body *be safe to relax, your* mind *be safe to flourish, and your* spirit *be safe to soar.*
*May you* reclaim *your breath, voice, gifts, and fire.*
*May you* glory *in the sound of your laughter and* delight *in the beauty of your dance.*

*May you forgive, accept, and love yourself* fully *and courageously.*

*May you recognize and* remember *yourself no matter what is happening around you.*

*May you give yourself permission to* always *come home and find the welcome mat in place.*

*May you connect with kindred spirits for* mutual *care along the way.*

*May the* sacredness *of your being always take priority over the busyness of your doing.*

*May you know deep down in your bones that you are* lovable *and worthy of* respect.

*May the values of compassion and* liberation *guide your feet in purposeful living.*

*May your soul perpetually tell your heart, mind, body, and spirit, "Welcome* home."

*Let it be so, and so it is.*

*Amen.*

## ADDITIONAL RESOURCES

**BOOKS**

Bourne, Edmond J. *The Anxiety and Phobia Workbook*. 7th ed. Oakland: New Harbinger Publications, 2020.

Bryant-Davis, Thema, ed. *Multicultural Feminist Therapy: Helping Adolescent Girls of Color to Thrive*. Washington, DC: American Psychological Association, 2019.

Bryant-Davis, Thema, and Lillian Comas-Díaz, eds. *Womanist and Mujerista Psychologies: Voices of Fire, Acts of Courage*. Washington, DC: American Psychological Association, 2016.

Comas-Díaz, Lillian, and Edil Torres Riveria, eds. *Liberation Psychology: Theory, Method, Practice, and Social Justice*. Washington, DC: American Psychological Association, 2020.

DeGruy, Joy. *Post Traumatic Slave Syndrome: America's Legacy of Enduring Injury and Healing*. Portland, OR: Joy DeGruy Publications Inc., 2017.

Delia, Lalah. *Vibrate Higher Daily: Live Your Power*. San Francisco: HarperOne, 2019.

Elle, Alexandra. *After the Rain: Gentle Reminders for Healing, Courage, and Self-Love*. San Francisco: Chronicle Books, 2020.

Gobin, Robyn L. *The Self-Care Prescription: Powerful Solutions to Manage Stress, Reduce Anxiety, and Increase Well-Being*. Emeryville: Althea Press, 2019.

Herman, Judith. *Trauma and Recovery: The Aftermath of Violence—from Domestic Abuse to Political Terror*. New York: Basic Books, 2015.

John, Jaiya. *Daughter Drink This Water: A Book of Sacred Love*. Soul Water Rising, 2018.

Kabat-Zinn, Jon. *Full Catastrophe Living: Using the Wisdom of Your Body and Mind to Face Stress, Pain, and Illness*. Revised edition. New York: Bantam, 2013.

Neville, Helen, Brendesha Tynes, and Shawn Utsey, eds. *Handbook of African American Psychology*. New York: Sage Publications, 2008.

Nichols, Morgan Harper. *All Along You Were Blooming: Thoughts for Boundless Living.* Grand Rapids: Zondervan, 2020.

Parker, Gail. *Restorative Yoga for Ethnic and Race-Based Stress and Trauma.* Philadelphia: Singing Dragon, 2020.

Shapiro, Francine. *Getting Past Your Past: Take Control of Your Life with Self-Help Techniques from EMDR Therapy.* New York: Rodale Books, 2013.

Singh, Anneliese. *The Racial Healing Handbook: Practical Activities to Help You Challenge Privilege, Confront Systemic Racism, and Engage in Collective Healing.* Oakland: New Harbinger Press, 2019.

Tawwab, Nedra Glover. *Set Boundaries, Find Peace: A Guide to Reclaiming Yourself.* New York: TarcherPerigee, 2021.

Taylor, Sonya Renee. *The Body Is Not An Apology: The Power of Radical Self-Love.* San Francisco: Berrett-Koehler Publishers, 2018.

Thurman, Howard. *Jesus and the Disinherited.* Boston: Beacon Press, 1996.

van der Kolk, Bessel. *The Body Keeps the Score: Brain, Mind, and Body in the Healing of Trauma.* New York: Viking, 2014.

Winfrey, Oprah, and Bruce Perry. *What Happened to You? Conversations on Trauma, Resilience, and Healing.* New York: Flatiron Books, 2021.

## THERAPY DIRECTORIES

Inclusive Therapists: www.inclusivetherapists.com
American Psychological Association: https://locator.apa.org
Therapy for Black Girls: www.therapyforblackgirls.com
The Association of Black Psychologists: https://abpsi.site-ym.com/
Latinx Therapy: www.latinxtherapy.com
Melanin & Mental Health: https://www.melaninandmentalhealth.com/

## PEER SUPPORT

National Alliance on Mental Illness—Support Services, Advocacy, Awareness Raising: https://www.nami.org/home

## MENTAL HEALTH CRISIS HOTLINE

Substance Abuse and Mental Health Services Administration (SAMSHA): 1-800-662-HELP (4357)
Rape, Abuse & Incest National Network (RAINN): 800-656-HOPE (4673)

## MEDITATION APPS

Shine

Stop, Breathe & Think

Calm

Liberate (created for the Black experience)

Abide (Christian)

## ACKNOWLEDGMENTS

I am grateful to God for the opportunity to share this work with you. Writing during a pandemic has been challenging and yet healing and empowering. I appreciate the time and space to do this work. I appreciate Bishop Vashti McKenzie for hosting the Selah women's retreat and inviting me to speak. Being among gifted, spiritual women inspired me to start *The Homecoming Podcast*. I am grateful for all of the listeners of the podcast around the world. Sharing with you is an honor, and hearing your responses motivated me to write this book.

I want to give a deep acknowledgment to my literary agent, Chris Park, whose consistent wisdom, compassion, and encouragement have been a welcome source of support on this journey. I appreciate your knowledge of the literary field as well as your spirit of both excellence and kindness. You are a gift.

I also wanted to share my great appreciation for Joanna Ng and the team at TarcherPerigee/Penguin Random House. From our first meeting and throughout this process, I have been overjoyed by the way in which you understand, appreciate, and care for my work. I am grateful to bring this project to life with your guidance and support.

I am so appreciative of Egypt Leithman and Brittany Jones for reading early versions of this manuscript and offering their insightful feedback.

I am so glad to have the support of my family and community without whom this work would not have been completed. Thank you for your loving presence, prayers, and encouragement. I want to thank my mother for encouraging me to write, my father for inspiring me to speak truth, and my brother for believing in me and reminding me to honor my unique voice. I want to thank "The Gathering," my sisterhood circle as well as my friends Edith, Rosalynn, and Amini. Your sisterhood is sacred and greatly appreciated.

Thank you to the clients I have worked with over the years. Your willingness to do the tender and yet challenging work of healing is remarkable. I am honored that you allowed me to walk with you on the journey.

Finally, thank you to all the readers for joining me on this journey. I hope you found some guideposts in these pages that will help you get home to your authentic self. You deserve it.

**Dr. Thema Bryant** is a clinical psychologist and an ordained minister in the African Methodist Episcopal Church. She is also a professor of psychology at Pepperdine University and a past American Psychological Association representative to the United Nations. She earned her doctorate from Duke University and completed her postdoctoral training at Harvard Medical Center. With over twenty years of experience in trauma recovery, Dr. Thema has appeared as a mental health expert on television, radio, and print media. She raises awareness about mental health issues on *The Homecoming Podcast* and her social media platforms.